LEADING MICKEY HOME

A Memoir

by Michael Leo Papesh

DORRANCE
PUBLISHING CO
EST. 1920
PITTSBURGH, PENNSYLVANIA 15238

Dorrance Publishing Co
585 Alpha Drive
Suite 103
Pittsburgh, PA 15238
Visit our website at *www.dorrancebookstore.com*

ISBN: 978-1-6491-3148-5
EISBN: 978-1-6491-3670-1

LEADING MICKEY HOME

A Memoir

To Dad, Mom, and Rog
and Gloria Ann Farkas (1931-2020)

When from our exile God leads us home again, we'll think we're dreaming ...

Home From Our Exile
Bernard Huijbers
after Psalm 126

CHAPTER I
A Death in Venice, Florida

"Mike? This is Roger. Dad died early this morning."

"What? What happened?" I asked, stunned by the abrupt news.

"I'm not sure. Lil called me at four-thirty California time, and I was only half awake. She said she was calling you."

"I haven't heard anything."

"You'd better call her. I think she's at Lynn's, but she could be going to the funeral home."

"Okay."

"The timing of this is a mess, Mike. Since I'm coming to Minnesota tomorrow it would be best if the funeral were Tuesday, then we can just drive down to Illinois." Of course. Our family's practical side always flowered fully no matter the emotions or circumstances.

"I would prefer Wednesday, Rog," I told him straightforwardly. The Archbishop was spending the weekend at the parish to make a pastoral visit and dedicate our new parish center on Sunday, which was why Roger was coming. Because of the elaborate preparations, I needed to keep my head and a steady hand on managing the details. I could switch into mourning only after the weekend was over. Presiding and preaching Dad's funeral would be delicate and demanding. "That gives me a little time to get through this weekend, then not only get there but also prepare." I had never done anything in my life without preparing.

"That's not good for me, Mike. I have to get back here as soon as I can to finish up work on the new building by the fifteenth, or I'll lose all my tenants." He had just purchased a three-unit apartment building near his home in the countryside south of San Jose for half a million dollars. His whole life was in hock. He had sixty days to get the building up to code. He planned to do all the work himself. As it was currently Thursday, May 31, a Minnesota visit and an Illinois funeral threatened his June 15 deadline.

Though he faced a pile of problems at home, Roger still extended me the great kindness of arranging to come to St. Paul for the dedication, even in the middle of his mess. He faced major work on the neglected new building. He also felt deeply rattled by his son Michael who had careened into crisis during the previous five months. Mike was caught having sex with his girlfriend and smoking marijuana, talked about suicide, called the police on Roger for abuse that never happened and cut down two trees in his high school's memorial garden. He faced a civil hearing and a likely fine from the tree cutting. Mike had also moved out of the house into his car. I'm certain all of these things were on Roger's mind as his stress spilled into panicked directness. "I prefer Tuesday," he said, voice tight.

I understood but immediately felt nervous. We were communicating at cross-purposes. "I'll call Lil and see what we can do, Rog. Since Mom and Joe are going to be here, maybe they can come to Illinois with us."

"Mike, you've got your administrative hat on," he responded. My stress was spilling on Roger and he was reacting. "Call Lil, then; let me know what's happening."

Rog and I learned from Dad that the first reaction to chaos was to bring about order. We learned well. We both had our administrative hats on. Rog felt as ill-at-ease with the surprise and the lack of smoothness about the details as I did. My role as older brother demanded that I manage things into some form of happy conclusion for us both.

"Okay. I'll talk to you later."

I put the receiver down, reeling from the surge of anxiety racing through me. I had just gotten back from breakfast with the deacons and, when the phone rang, was passing through the house briefly to let the two dogs out. It was a quarter to ten. I was scheduled to meet the deacons to pre-rehearse the Sunday building dedication in fifteen minutes, then meet with the parish staff for a last-minute briefing at tent-thirty, then meet with the servers at eleven o'clock for a rehearsal. Mom and Joe were due in around three o'clock. I still had some straightening to do around the rectory and needed to purchase cabbage for coleslaw. Now this.

I called the business administrator. "Mary? Mike. My Dad died this morning."

"Oh, Mike, I'm sorry."

"Thanks, Mary. Please tell the deacons that I cannot make the pre-rehearsal. Then please conduct the staff meeting without me. I need to make a few phone calls right now. I will be on hand to rehearse with the servers and the deacons at eleven o'clock."

"Mike, just do what you need to do."

"Mary, please keep things moving forward. I'll be on hand in church at eleven o'clock."

"Okay. Don't worry about a thing," she responded. I felt completely confident Mary could handle anything.

To sweep my internal mess into a single pile if possible, I took the dogs out for a brief walk. The day shone bright, clear, and comfortable. Asher, the boxer, and Reji, the Boston terrier, excitedly gamboled about as always. They served as perfect company. Meanwhile, my head was swimming. The rehearsals, reviewing final preparations, Mom, Joe, and Roger coming, the Archbishop on hand for the weekend, the ceremonies on Sunday, the reception, the accumulated stress of the new building, the parish community in tumult for three months, and now this. "Wow, Lord, you can really pile it on," I prayed. "I guess I can handle it, but wow!"

I sang the Introit of the Latin Requiem Mass to myself as a way of praying for Dad, tiptoeing into the event of his dying, and starting to bring reality home. I ended with the Kyrie. I loved the Requiem as a child. In seventh and eighth grade, our class served as the choir for most funerals at my home parish. Dad was often the funeral director. I even played the organ for it once during daily Mass at St. Joe's. Nervous, I played very badly. I crashed. But still, through all the years, the Requiem's music and words offered comfort. I also let my mind run regarding what Scripture readings might be selected for Dad's funeral and what I might say. I had thought about both for years. Now was the time to pull it together, but my thoughts flew like kites in a March wind.

Back at the rectory, I let the dogs off their leashes to run in the yard and then went to the phone to call Lil's daughter, Lynn, in North Aurora, Illinois. A machine answered. I left a message. "Lil? Michael. Roger called me about Dad. I'm trying to get a hold of you. I will keep trying. My prayers are with you."

I then called Dad's sister, Gloria. It occurred to me that she might know Lil's whereabouts. I left a message on her machine. "Gloria? Michael. I heard about Dad. I'm looking for Lil. I will be in touch with you later today. My sympathies to you."

Then I called Lil's brother's home. I had only met Bill Kobe and his family once some years ago. I thought the call worth a try.

"Hello."

"Hello, is this Charlene?" Char was Bill's wife.

"Yes?"

"Charlene, this is Michael Papesh. I am looking for Lil. Is she there by chance?"

"No, she isn't. I think she is at Lynn's."

"I have tried, but there was no answer."

4

"Well, if she calls here, I will tell her you are looking for her."

"Thank you."

"Goodbye." That felt curt and chilly – odd.

I then called Fred C. Dames Funeral Home in Joliet. The secretary put Jeff Dames on the phone. Jeff's father, Mark, was Dad's former colleague and probably the person Dad would have considered his best friend the last twenty-five years. When Mark and Sharon vacationed in Florida, Dad and Lil dined and drank with them. Jeff was Mark and Sharon's oldest son. I had seen him once, thirty years ago, a buck-toothed ten-year-old blonde with curls.

"My sympathies to you, Father."

"Thank you, Jeff. I am calling to see if perhaps Lillian is there."

"No, Father, she's not. We have not heard from her for a while now."

"Jeff, have any arrangements been made?"

"Yes, Father, the arrangements are made. They can be changed, of course. Nothing is in stone."

I was taken aback. My expectation was that we would have made arrangements as a family together. Fearing that the decisions made would be screwy and I would soon have hard work to do, I felt my bile rising. "What are they, Jeff?"

"Your father will be waked next Friday. The funeral will be Saturday."

"Eight days from now?"

"Yes, Father. Lillian wanted some time to go down to Florida to see your father, pick up some things and then come back for the wake and funeral. She is trying to arrange flights."

"Hmm." Lil had gone to Illinois to see her mother and family during the past two weeks. I gathered she felt guilty and self-preoccupied that she had not been with Dad when he died. It seemed her emotions were leading her to increase her stress enormously.

"Then the body will be cremated Saturday afternoon."

I couldn't hold back the hiss that escaped my lips, the sound like when you touch your hand to a burning fry pan. "Father?" Jeff asked.

"I am sorry, Jeff. Were it my choice," I said with firm heat, "I would never have a member of my family cremated. Ever."

"Yes, Father." He kept cool. "These are the pre-arrangements Lillian made."

My suspicions were growing dark. "Do you know when, Jeff?"

"I believe my father and Lillian agreed to these in early 2000," Jeff responded.

Dad was diagnosed with Alzheimer's in 1995. At that time, he told me he had just made pre-arrangements. He was so direct that everything was settled that I assumed that he was informing me I had no control. That was certainly the message I got. By early 2000, he was in a nursing home, confined to a wheelchair, mumbling to himself. Dad had not made these pre-arrangements.

"I also understand, Father," Jeff went on, "that there is very little money. Lillian was thinking about having your father cremated in Florida, but we agreed to pay to have his body brought up to Illinois. She says these arrangements are the best she can do."

Not *that* little money, I thought. She evidently presumed Roger and I would stay out. That thought made me wince. "When is the burial?" I asked.

"The burial will be the following Monday."

"Monday!" I blurted out. I couldn't believe what I heard. She was thinking of no one, even herself, it seemed.

"Father," Jeff said kindly but firmly, "after the cremation on Saturday afternoon it would not be possible to bury the ashes before Monday. These are the arrangements Lillian made. She is the legal next-of-kin. Your father's body will not be arriving here until Sunday evening, or perhaps Monday. There is time for these arrangements to change if the family wishes. However, Lillian is the legal next-of-kin and she must authorize any changes."

"Thank you, Jeff." His clarity about the responsibilities was, if challenging, immensely helpful. I appreciated his professionalism. Dad would have, too.

But I still felt irritated, out-of-sorts. "Tell me, Jeff, since so much of this has been decided already, are there any specifications about the funeral Mass, like who is presiding or who is preaching?" Poor Jeff didn't deserve my sarcasm. Though the question was germane, I was spilling.

"Just a moment, Father." There was a brief pause. "No. There are no specifications about the funeral Mass except that it be at St. Joe's."

"Thank you. I thought I ought to check that out since so very much has been arranged without my brother and I being consulted." Another spill, this time hurt and anger, with the boiling mercury of pomposity.

"Again, Father, any of these arrangements can be changed as long as the changes are authorized by Lillian as legal next-of-kin." Jeff was adamantly professional. I liked that.

Feeling embarrassed by my anger, I decided to rise above it to gather some information. "Jeff, what would the difference in cost be between cremation and burying Dad whole?"

"I would need to do a little research on that, Father."

"Could it be done for, say, $2,000 or so?"

"Yes, I think so, but I would have to get back to you. I would not be able to give you a quote off the top of my head."

"Great, Jeff. Do that. I would like to see what's possible."

"I will get back to you, Father. Probably around noon or so."

"Thank you, Jeff. If I miss your call, I will be in touch with you as soon as I can."

I couldn't wait to call Roger.

"Mike, that's nuts!" Roger exclaimed upon hearing the news. "Lil expects me to fly to Minnesota, fly back to California, then four days later fly to Illinois for Dad's funeral, then fly back again? I would only be able to stay overnight for the funeral. I couldn't be at the burial at all. I don't have time. I have work to do. And then who is going to pay all this airfare?"

I noted with some pleasure that his time in Minnesota seemed to be a higher priority for him than Dad's funeral.

"I will call Lil, Rog, and see if she will make other arrangements." I felt amazed that I remained very much 'the professor' to his 'the clown.' Roger never liked the designation Dad gave us at four and two, but we lived it. Besides, I felt adamant that the arrangements needed to change, and knew I had the tact to get at least most of the way toward what Rog and I preferred.

"You've got to, Mike. That schedule is crazy."

"What do you think about cremation, Rog?" I wanted to see if we were together on the subject. A little brass box of ashes and Dad had nothing in common from my perspective. Because cremation defied the Christian notion of the sacredness of the human body, and because the picture of the event itself in my head smacked of unspeakable cruelty, I felt repelled by cremation.

"Dad would not want to be incinerated, Mike. Where'd that come from?" Clearly Roger agreed and with similar vehemence.

"Jeff says that Dad's pre-arrangements were changed. Evidently Lil and Mark Dames worked these arrangements out in early 2000. Money is the reason, and Lil is the legal next-of-kin, so she's in charge. Dad would never want to be cremated, unless maybe he said something while he was depressed or in one of his 'what-the-hell-do-I-care-and-who-gives-a-damn-anyway' moods. He always expected to be buried whole. But Rog, would you be willing to help pay for it if arrangements could be different?"

"What would it cost?"

"I asked Jeff if it could be done on a budget of $2,000. Could you pay half of that do you think?"

"Oh, well," he said with a resigned sigh. "I am spending money like water right now anyway."

"It could cost a little more. How about $2,500?"

"I would like to keep it closer to a $1,000 for me."

"I'll call Jeff and Lil and see what's possible. I would prefer to bury Dad whole and I think that's what he would want."

"Mike, make sure to use that phrase 'bury him whole.' That should get to her," he said with a chuckle. Roger was always the streetwise one.

It was eleven o'clock, time for the dedication servers' practice. The two deacons, four servers, the master of ceremonies, and the liturgy director were all on hand when I arrived, ready to go. I felt somewhat numb, reeling emotionally inside. The practice, the best thing for me at the time, went well. For as complex as the ceremony was – moving from the Liturgy of the Word in the church to the commons of the new building for the blessing, then from the commons to the new gym for the Liturgy of the Eucharist – we had encapsulated the ceremony into workable parts for everyone. The Archbishop's preferences regarding the miter and crosier were the only mystery left. The appointed team was our best.

After the practice, I went to the parish office to pick-up my messages. I found one from Lil left at six-thirty that morning. She asked me to call her, saying it was important. I wondered why she called me at the office rather than at home. Jeff Dames had left a message, too. I immediately telephoned him.

"Well, Father, this is what we can do," Jeff said, answering my call immediately. "We can provide a nice wood casket for $2,000. Opening the grave would cost another $1,000. A vault would cost $335. That would bring the total bill to $3,335. If we use a concrete box rather than a sealing vault, that cuts the cost $200. If your stepmother spends the same amount as she is currently planning, that reduces the expenses another $600 or so."

"I would like the casket to have a mahogany finish. Does it have that?"

"No, Father, but what I have here is very nice. In fact, I think it looks better than the mahogany finish, which is a little more expensive. It has the Last Supper on the handles." Eight Last Suppers around the casket sounded like kitsch to me, but Jeff was a salesman talking to a priest.

"Does the vault versus the concrete box matter?"

"No, Father, it's simply what you prefer. The cemetery requires only the concrete box."

"That's $3,335, huh?"

"Father, that's with the casket at our cost. Mike was like family to us. He taught me a lot as a kid. I remember him standing there with his arms folded as I learned to wash cars, pointing out where I had missed. He was the only one who ever worked for Dames' whom we trusted alone in the building. My parents have a great deal of respect for him."

Though he intended to convey respect and affection, Jeff's remarks struck me as patronizing and arrogant. He deserved wide berth, however, if some reserve.

"Thank you, Jeff. I appreciate your kindness." I had mastered my father's casket-side manner a long time ago.

"Father, when we were talking to Lillian, she wasn't sure how many graves were left at St. Joseph's Cemetery in the Papesh plot. Is it two or three?"

"Three. Two for Dad and Lil, one for me."

"Thanks, Father. That helps. I will check with the cemetery anyway, just to be sure."

"Okay, Jeff. Let me talk with my brother and I will get back to you."

"We will need authorization from Lillian, Father," he gently reminded me.

"I understand, Jeff. I will let you know one way or the other. You may also be getting a call from Lil. I don't know."

"I am happy to be of help, Father. Call me if you need anything."

I went back across the street to the rectory for a quiet lunch. Asher and Reji ran about the yard playing. I brought them in. They had biscuits and water while I ate a tuna salad sandwich with a pickle, cottage cheese, and some potato chips. Worn, I let my mind run. I wondered about readings, about what to preach. I didn't know what to make of it that I felt no sadness. Glad to be away from everyone, I hummed the Requiem as I did the dishes.

I went upstairs to rest before checking my mail and making a run to the grocery store. Mom and Joe were due at three o'clock, but I needed to lay down. I had a little time.

The phone rang. "Well, hello there. How are ya'?" It was Gloria. Almost six years younger than Dad, her ebullience and directness contrasted sharply with Dad's reserve and politeness, much like tavern keeper Grandpa contrasted with church lady Grandma. Gloria had been at work, her retirement job of sitting with senior citizens. She had just gotten home.

"Hi, Gloria. My sympathies to you."

"Thank you, Michael. Isn't it sad?"

"Yes, it is. But he was a proud peacock of a man and this is better than his sitting in a wheelchair mumbling – for him and for Lil."

"Yeah, but it's still sad."

"Yeah, it is. Gloria, do you know what's happening?"

"Nothing. I got a call early this morning. Lil said she was going to call the boys. That's it." I could hear her sadness.

I explained the arrangements as I understood them and how I got them. Her only remark during the explanation was a slow, drawn out, "Michael, a rented casket?"

We were a proud family. I knew that would gall her.

When I finished, she said, "Well, Michael, I don't know what to say. I guess I just have to stay out of it. She's in charge. I don't know why she is poor mouthing to the Dames', though. After all that time with Mark and Sharon in Florida you'd think she'd have more self-respect. Isn't that sad?"

"Yeah."

"She tol' me this morning that Tina was with him last night, but she felt bad that he died alone." There was an emphatic pause. "Michael, no one dies alone."

"Yes, that's true," I replied. I was used to Gloria's edginess about Lil but felt surprised to hear such depth of religious conviction from her. Gloria had given me pause many times during the last twenty-five years of Dad's and Lil's marriage, though.

"Gloria, I am going to try and get a hold of Lil to touch base and see how she is doing. If I can, I will try to change the arrangements. We'll see what happens. Meanwhile, I just wanted you to know where things stand right now. I will let you know if there's anything further."

"Well, I'm here!"

I laid down for twenty minutes, then went downstairs to spend twenty minutes at the kitchen table fingering through the Book of Tobit. Since burying the dead was what got Tobit in trouble, and Dad had spent his life doing the same, I thought I might find a suitable passage for the first reading. I didn't.

I went back upstairs to dress, then back downstairs to my home office to call Roger. It was a quarter to three. I explained to Rog all that Jeff had explained to me.

"Things are a little open-ended because I am not sure what Lil is willing to do, Rog. But it could cost us nearly $1,700 apiece."

"Well, Mike, just play it out and we'll see what happens. I would like it to stay closer to a $1,000, but oh well."

I heard telltale noises. "Mom and Joe just pulled in," I told him. I looked outside and saw both car doors open and Joe standing at the trunk.

Mom was coming up the back steps with a clothes bag in her hands, leaning forward as she always did when climbing steps, with a smile on her face and a look of gleeful expectation. A shrinking five-feet-one, Mary Jean Beaudry Papesh Arado was a healthy about-to-be-seventy-five. Fighting weight all her life, Mom called herself "a pear," remarkably small on top and large on the bottom. She developed cloaking her shape with her clothing into a high art form, wearing her steel-gray hair short and curly, usually attired in a vest or jacket with slacks, never without make-up, earrings, and a necklace. Her physical stamina lagging some, her psychological stamina remained formidable, determined. Her grit served as both boon and burden to the passion of her life, her two sons. She was Ireland itself in wit and love of laughter.

"Let me talk to Mom," Rog said firmly.

"Rog, please don't tell her yet. Let me handle it here."

"I won't. Just let me talk to her."

"Mom, it's Rog," I said, and I handed her the phone. She put the bags down on the spot and dove in with Roger while walking to the first floor living room couch. I went downstairs and out the door to greet Joe at the car.

I found Joe standing at the open trunk and we immediately embraced. Somewhat taller than Mom, Joe was stocky but stayed thin – courtesy of a cancer operation in 1978 in which his stomach was removed. Bald, dark-haired, gray at the temples, and graced with an egg-shaped head, large at the top, Joe presented a classically Italian hooked nose and a wide, heavy-lipped, Polish smile. Small hands and stubby fingers also bespoke his Polish heritage, as well as a lifetime of gardening and six years of hay ranching in Colorado. Penetrating eyes and a pensive look suggested his half-century of playing hard and winning on the stock market. Self-willed, patriotic, and a man of strong opinions, Joe worked for what he wanted and got it, a Jeffersonian to his bone marrow.

13

I grabbed a couple of bags and we ascended the stairs. We stopped at the living room door, dropped everything in the hallway, and went in to sit down as Mom finished with Roger.

"How's Roger?" Joe began, turning to Mom.

"Oh, he's all upset about Michael. He just goes on and on about Michael." She turned to me sitting next to her on the couch, "Hi, Mike!" she said, and she reached up her arms and drew my head to hers for a kiss.

"Hi, Mom," I responded mid-pull. "How was the trip?"

"Oh, it was pretty good," Joe began. Then he listed off the military bases where they had stayed, an earned privilege of thirty years' service for a retired weekend warrior Navy captain. They filled me in on the accommodations and the food.

Mom then turned to me with chatty zest, asking, "How are you, Mike?"

"Well, I have been better. Dad died in the early hours of this morning."

"What? Oh, Michael, I am sorry," she said, and she drew me to herself again.

"I am sorry, Mike. What happened?" Joe asked.

"Well, I think it was most likely a stroke. I am not sure. I haven't talked with Lil yet. But given the kind of Alzheimer's he had I suspect it was likely the last of a series of strokes."

"Well, the timing couldn't be worse, could it? With all this going on here?" Mom observed.

"Frankly, the timing couldn't be better," I retorted.

Mom went wide-eyed.

"Who would have imagined that I would have you and Roger here at a time like this?" I went on. "We haven't been all together in Minnesota since my ordination in 1983."

"Mike, don't tell anyone you think that. They'll think you're hardhearted." Mom was always concerned about what others thought but never pushed if she thought her opinion the simple truth. She let go. "What's going to happen?"

I filled them in on the arrangements as I knew them and on the multiple conversations with family and Jeff Dames. They agreed that the arrangements seemed maximally inconvenient, nutty in fact. They supported Roger's and my intention to get things changed.

"You know, Mike, your father would never want to be cremated. He spent his life as a funeral director, and he wanted the best. Not only that, he would want all those Slovenians in Joliet to see the best. Appearances were everything. That's all her – and the reason is money." Then, like the good Irish lass she was, Mom's grudges reared. "Besides, you'd think the Dames' would buy him a casket for all he has done for them."

"I know. Roger and I have agreed that we will pay for burying him whole. Roger wants me to be sure to use that phrase when I talk to Lil."

"Oh, yeah," Joe said. "That's the right thing."

"Right," Mom chimed in. "You won't be able to live with your-self unless you try to do your best. If she won't change it, at least you've tried."

"Well," Joe interrupted. "Where are we staying?" He never waxed content with bad news for very long, or our family news for that matter. He either changed the subject or left the room. At the moment he wanted to do both.

I showed them the newly redone bedroom downstairs off the living room, which Joe favored. He moved things right in. Mom wanted to settle in upstairs and said so. I decided to let them work it out.

I went across the street to the offices to check mail and phone calls. I found little of either. I decided to let go of the coleslaw since we were going out to eat anyway.

By the time I got back from across the street, Mom and Joe were lugging suitcases upstairs. "She's the boss," Joe said on the steps.

"Well, I have always stayed in the room at the top of the steps when I am here, and I like it. I am comfortable there. Besides, it really doesn't make any difference."

"Mom, if it doesn't make any difference why not stay downstairs?"

Joe looked up at me with a twinkle in his eye for daring to say the obvious.

"He-e-y!" she said with her hands on her hips.

We all laughed, and they moved in upstairs.

CHAPTER II
Re-Arrangements 1:
There is a Time to Mourn

Mom, Joe, and I had five-thirty reservations at Buca di Beppo, a syndicated Italian restaurant that served too much food selected off a painted wood menu mounted on the wall. The food was Southern Italian, Joe's exclusive preference, and Joe enjoyed Buca's. It also served a fantastic tiramisu.

Once we arrived, we had to ask management to turn down the air conditioning for Mom. We all agreed on – what were for Joe – the non-negotiable raviolis, and then we also selected another entree. I had some Chianti, which I felt justified in ordering since I intended to treat. When I managed to snatch the bill before Joe did, I had to promise him that he could pay on Sunday night, when we were planning to come back again with Roger. We aimed to celebrate Mom's birthday that night, though she didn't know that yet. Joe paid for too much, but I acquiesced to his insistence that no alternative existed to his paying on Sunday. We walked out with a shopping bag of leftovers.

For most of the meal, we talked about the awkward funeral arrangements and speculated about Lil's motives and real interests. It was a conversation going nowhere, really. Joe seemed less than excited about the topic, but Dad's death was momentous for us all, even Joe.

Mom felt keenly engaged in every detail and had opinions to share on everything.

•   •   •

When Roger and I were sixteen and eighteen, Mom decided to buff-up her secretarial skills and apply for a job at the Elgin, Joliet & Eastern Railway in Joliet. Because her grandfather had been superintendent of "the J" in the 1920s, three uncles and an aunt had worked there, and her father had worked there for years, Mom had no difficulty getting a job there in 1943 when she graduated from high school. She remained at "the J" until I was born in 1950. So, when Mom decided to return to the work force in December 1968, "the J" was the only place she even considered. After three years in the Accounting Department, she was hired in the Industrial Development and Real Estate Department by its Director, Joseph E. Arado.

In 1971, Joe, three years Mom's junior, was a married man with a thirteen-year-old son. He spent his weekends as a Navy Reserve Commander in the field of intelligence and his vacations in Washington, D.C. at the Pentagon. By mid-1973, Joe was facing up to his unhappy marriage. That fall, he started to express interest in Mom with ever-increasing attention, little gifts, and, for Mom, the very big words, "I like you."

Mom's reaction was, "Don't like me." Her marriage and family circumstances, however, left her vulnerable.

Dad was consumed by funeral direction work. His relationship with Mom centered on sex. He was ever ready to show his volatile, if short-lived, temper, and, insistent on having his own way, Dad had alienated Mom emotionally years before. I think it unlikely that he knew it. Mom, rather naive, fulfilled her actress responsibilities in the bedroom and followed through on all else that she assumed went with marriage. She compensated for whatever alienation she felt from Dad by focusing her life on Roger and me, extended family, church work, and neighborhood friends. Ultimately, Mom decided to go back to work for financial reasons. Mom and Dad needed two incomes to fund college for us.

Underestimating the underlying boredom yawning between them, I assumed at the time that Mom and Dad remained content. The fabric that had held them together for many years, however, had grown flimsy, for Mom especially.

I boarded at school starting in 1967, was away at college after 1970, and then entered a monastery in 1972. In high school and college, Roger considerably strained Mom and Dad's marriage, at least that's the way Dad saw it. One summer evening, for instance, Rog took to painting black the interior of a new blue American Motors Javelin. Dad imploded. "Mary Jean, tell him get that paint off. If I go downstairs to the basement work room, I'll kill him."

Mom, afraid, obliged.

Dad remained convinced that Roger fell short as college material. Mom was determined that Roger get a college education. Roger's high energy and impulsive unpredictability, combined with the ordinary 1970s college fare of girlfriends, sex, drugs, cars, and seemingly endless opportunities for truancy, kept Mom and Dad in almost continual stress and disagreement over Roger.

When Dad insisted on moving to a new home in 1970, Mom resisted, but lost the battle. Fading neighbor relationships had gone into eclipse. Time with the extended family had diminished because of deaths and parental absorption in their children. At the same time Grandma Foster, Mom's mother and something of a vampire, increased her many-times-a-day intrusions into family life, which added stress. Returning to the workforce had also curtailed Mom's church work.

Joe's attentions, intensely focused personal caring, and stiff resolution to conquer, exposed the fabric of Mom's life to be nearly threadbare. Dependent by disposition, lonely, feeling used by Dad sexually, and deeply confused, Mom's vulnerability offered fertile ground for Joe's wooing. His divorce from his wife in February 1974 trebled the pressure.

Dad became aware of Joe's interest and Mom's vulnerability through a tip from one of Mom's cousins, Otts Stoiber, and then from a phone call to his employer's mother, Mrs. Dames. Only later did we find out that Mom's mother had made the call to Mrs. Dames, insinuating a liaison.

Dad's response was probably the worst possible. Slovenian pessimism and self-pity led him to tell his mother and sister about it, then, through Gloria, to have the house appraised. That shook Mom's fragile sense of security even as it inflamed her age-old resentments toward Dad's family. Pushed by the situation to take a stand about his feelings toward Mom and his desire for her, Dad's pride and Slovenian melancholy streak combined to lead him ultimately to step back. He told Mom she needed to make her own decision between him and Joe.

One evening, Joe surprised Mom and Dad both by dropping in at the house wearing Navy dress whites. Dad sat with him around our kitchen table as Joe made his case for Mom and asked Dad to step back. Joe was firm and impassioned. Rather than throw Joe out of the house for his arrogance, Dad maintained his politeness and his ambivalent she-is-free-to-choose-whom-she-wants posture. Mom felt wholly discombobulated.

I stumbled into the turmoil when I called home from the monastery – where I was then living – on Sunday, April 14, 1974, to wish everyone a happy Easter. Mom and Dad were both on the phone. Something was amiss.

"What's going on?" I asked. "The two of you don't sound like yourselves."

"Nothing," Mom said.

"Really? Hmm. You don't sound quite right."

"Let's just say 'domestic problems,'" Dad responded.

"Domestic problems!" To my mind that was code for divorce. "What do you mean, domestic problems?"

"I'll let your mother explain it to you."

"Michael, I am going to divorce your father." I was shocked, stunned, sent reeling. "We didn't want to tell you on the phone. We wanted to wait and tell you personally. I am sorry about that. Would you be willing to come home and talk with us about it?"

"Yes, Son, maybe you could help," Dad cut in. "Your mother needs someone to talk some sense into her."

Instantly and instinctively, I knew that I could be of no help refereeing their relationship. Immature and deeply confused myself, I had far too many problems of my own.

"No. Send Roger." I desperately needed to talk about what was happening. Only Roger would do. After asking me if I was sure, they agreed to send him down to Southern Indiana.

During the week following, through phone calls and letters, I got something of the lay of the land from each of them. I felt suspended over a black abyss with a massive hook in my guts.

Roger arrived the next Friday night. In the car from the airport I was surprised to learn that our historical roles with Mom and Dad had reversed. I, historically a mama's boy, felt furious with her. He, always a daddy's helper, supported Mom. After a weekend of talk with each other and one of the monks, Roger and I called Mom and Dad on Sunday just prior to Roger's leaving to fly home. On the phone together, we told them that we would remain neutral. Their relationship was theirs. We urged them to get the help they needed but clarified that we were not it. We could do nothing to help them work out their relationship.

They, we learned later, were crushed. Mom and Dad both felt abandoned.

Joe's wooing continued unabated.

Mom soon decided to quit "the J." Dad had never once suggested it. Because he evidently wanted the money, despite the relationship stakes, he felt ambivalent about her leaving the job. Mom saw quitting as the only way out. She placed resignation letters in Joe's desk and those of her other supervisors on a Saturday. Talking with Roger on the side about all that was going on – Roger worked in the yard crew at "the J" and, knowing no strangers, knew Joe – Joe telephoned him for a report on Mom and learned from Roger about Mom's resignation letters. Joe went to the office on Sunday, retrieved the letters, then talked Mom out of leaving the job. Her confusion became thoroughgoing.

After months of restrained ambivalence and self-pity as he waited for Mom to decide what to do, and despising the wait, Dad's temper began to spill out. His sexual demands of Mom increased, and he became verbally taunting and physically threatening. In the mounting pressure of his crushing disappointment at Mom's continuing affair, his inability to elicit clear intentions from her, and feeling internally restless, anxious to get Mom to decide, Dad exploded one evening and put Mom out of the house onto the front stoop in her nightgown. He aimed the action toward giving Mom an albeit rude but pointed reality check. He wanted her to see, feel and experience what her dalliance was doing to their relationship and her relationship with the whole family.

In her muddled self-preoccupation, Mom missed Dad's point and felt pushed away. Dad's methods outraged and scared her. Mom moved out over the next days – by May 9 in fact. Joe found Mom an apartment, with a roommate, a few miles from his own place in DuPage County. Motivated partly by his pride in himself as a provider and partly by wanting to quell E. J. & E. company gossip, Joe insisted Mom quit her job. Joe also immediately engaged an attorney for Mom and took the lead in working with him to procure Mom a speedy divorce. By June 20, on the grounds of physical and mental abuse, proven by pictures of bruises on Mom's arms, Mom and Dad were divorced.

Afterward alone and disoriented as she faced a whole new life of she knew-not-what, Mom languished. Forty miles away from anything familiar, Mom was left with nothing to do but try to settle emotionally, figure out a way to save face, and get to know Joe at his place after his work day and on weekends. I remember distinctly Mom calling me at the monastery during those days to ask if I would come to their wedding. Even the thought of her being married to someone I had never met felt jarring and unimaginable; I told her no. I learned years later, however, that at the time she called, Mom and Joe had no concrete plans. Joe was dragging his feet about getting married because he felt ambivalent about a permanent commitment and worried about the reaction of his sixteen-year-old son.

By early August, Mom decided that her situation left her too much at risk. After all she had been through, she wanted security. Mom told Joe one Friday evening, "Hey, if this is going to go on, then we have to get married."

The next morning, Saturday, August 2, Joe drove Mom to the courthouse at McHenry County, Illinois, found an official and a couple of witnesses, and they got hitched. On the drive over to the courthouse, Joe stopped off at a Service Merchandise store to buy a diamond ring, with Mom watching.

Now, in these days, Dad's death was raising up all that past. I was learning for myself what I had long observed in families I had helped prepare for funerals. At the time of death, all a family's history and pathology gets scooped out of hiding and splashed on the table for everyone's final review.

•   •   •

When we returned to the rectory, I decided to try Lil again. I excused myself, leaving Mom and Joe in the living room. I called Lynn's.

"Hi, Mike," Lynn said, answering the phone. "Mom's right here."

After a few seconds of silence, Lil picked up the line.

"Hello-o."

I could hear her grief and fatigue. "Hello, Lil. Michael. I am sorry about Dad."

"Thanks, Michael. I felt so bad not being with him. After three years of not seeing my mom, I leave and this happens. He was okay when I left."

"Lil, don't blame yourself for that. You needed the break. We all encouraged you to take the break after all you had been through, especially taking care of him at home for so long. Besides, given when he died, you probably wouldn't have been with him, even if you were in Florida."

"That's what Lynn says."

"Listen to her. I think she is right. You are exactly where you need to be for now."

"And then there's all these arrangements. I have a ticket to leave on Saturday, but I am having trouble getting a ticket back in time for the wake."

"Why are you going back to Florida, Lil?"

"I want to see him and get some clothes for him. I don't have a dress here that I can wear, either."

"Lil, I can't imagine that you don't have *something* you can wear," I said, slightly exasperated. Her focus on her appearance was always riveted.

"I also have some things to do. I am just so exhausted I don't know what I am doing. I am feeling confused, and so tired."

That was my entryway in, so I took it. "Lil, it sounds to me as if you are setting yourself up for the most stressful circumstances possible. Why don't you call Tina, have her get Dad a black suit, a yellow tie, shoes, socks, and underwear, and get them to the funeral home. Then you can just rest and prepare yourself to receive him here."

"But I have things to do at home."

"Like what?"

"I have to bring in the mail. I don't have any cash with me, no money."

"Can't the mail wait?"

"It's been three weeks."

"If it's already been three weeks, can't it wait another four or five days? And if you have a charge card with you, money is no problem. Besides, I should think Lynn would be happy to help if necessary."

"That's what she says. Oh, I don't know. And then I can't get a plane back until midnight Thursday."

"Lil, all this has happened this way for a reason. You are with the best person in the world for you to have support and comfort. You need time. You need rest. Please have Tina or someone else get Dad's clothes. Just rest and prepare yourself to receive him on Monday or Tuesday before a wake and funeral mid-week. You can have time alone with him when he comes here."

"That's what Lynn says. I don't know. I am so confused."

I knew I had just one shot and she had just given me another opening. "Lil, would it be all right if I talked with Lynn?"

"Okay. She's right here."

Another few seconds of silence, and then Lynn spoke up. "Hello, Mike?"

"Hi, Lynn. Lynn, this is the oldest to the oldest. Got it?" Two years older than me, I knew I could rely on Lynn both to receive and be a straight shot.

"Got it."

"Lynn, your mom going back to Florida puts the maximum possible stress on her, and she needs the opposite of that right now."

"I think so, too. I told her that."

"Lynn, can't Tina get Dad a black suit, yellow tie, shoes, socks, and underwear and get it to the funeral home? Then your mom could receive him here when he comes, and we can have the wake and funeral Monday and Tuesday, or Tuesday and Wednesday."

"I agree with you. I think that's a good idea."

"There's another reason, Lynn. Roger is flying in tomorrow from California to attend the dedication for a new building here. It seems crazy for him to fly back Monday to have him fly to Illinois on Thursday or Friday. He will already be here. We are all here. If the funeral were earlier in the week we could just drive down from here and we would all be together."

"I think that makes sense." Her flat Chicago twang on the vowels was amazing to hear. Home.

"Lynn, if it's at all possible, I would prefer to have the funeral Wednesday so I can get through things here and have time to drive down, make arrangements with St. Joe's, and prepare."

"I'll talk with Mom about that. I think it's right."

"Lynn, another thing. I think it ought to be a yellow tie. Yellow was Dad's favorite color." Dad was fastidious about his appearance. Even as a teen during the Depression, Dad always stood out, Mom said. His shirts were pressed, his pants creased. He would watch, but never participate in games with the other guys because he wanted to keep his clothes clean. His slacks could be blue, red, or white. He even had a pair of yellow slacks in those years.

"A yellow tie? Oh, okay. We'll take care of that."

"Thanks, Lynn."

"Mom's under so much stress, Mike. I think we just need to be sensible about this thing. She is very tired and needs rest. We'll talk about it and probably call tomorrow morning."

"Okay. Thanks, Lynn. I appreciate this very much."

"Oh, you're welcome."

She immediately hung up the phone. It was now in Lynn's hands, and Lil's.

I called Roger to let him know what was, or maybe wasn't, achieved thus far. He listened, and then gave his two cents: "Mike, it sounds like Lil is all goofed up right now. I am leaving for the airplane at six-thirty tomorrow morning, so I'll be unavailable all day. Do what you can."

When I reached the living room, Joe asked, "Well, what's the verdict?"

"I find out tomorrow." Then I told the story.

"She probably has to get a new change of clothes and have her hair done. That's why she wants to go back to Florida." Mom always managed to deliver cattiness, leaving the impression it was dogma.

"Now, Mom. You're probably right but let's be nice."

Then something struck me about the whole day that I would not have expected. "You know what the strangest thing is about all this? I have talked with Lil, Lynn, Gloria, and Charlene Kobe. I have extended my sympathy to all of them. None of them has expressed their sympathy to me. Not one."

Mom responded crisply, "Well, they've listened to twenty-five years of old stories, that's why!"

•　　•　　•

Over twenty-five years, all I knew about Lil or her family came from Dad. Lil herself, while always pleasant and courteous to me, never revealed much. She carefully stood back when I was around. Over the years I gathered that her reserve came from three perceptions. She believed a father should have time with his son; she once told me she thought Dad and I needed that. She likely felt mildly intimidated and self-conscious because I was a priest. I also suspect that she saw lurking in me under the surface Dad's straightforward and wide-eyed clarity when push came to shove.

Dad told me during their dating that Lil had been deeply hurt by life. Though she was the elder, Lil's brother, Billy, was stoutly favored by Lil's parents. Lil had a strong relationship with Billy, but especially her father's attitude toward her left Lil feeling very second fiddle within her own family all her life, Dad said. I sensed that in her myself through Lil's consistent self-conscious reserve even as she presented herself to the world as a smart, classy, even evocative dresser. Mom cattily commented after Dad remarried that Lil had been a sleep-around in high school and had a reputation for continuing that after marriage. Whatever may have occurred in high school, Dad confided that Lil found herself in a loveless marriage to an overly busy, aloof car salesman. They had two daughters together early in their marriage but had no sex life at all for over sixteen years until they divorced. Furthermore, Lil's younger daughter had run Lil through the ringer of truancy, sex, and drugs misbehavior over many years. Devoted and a worrier, Lil felt angered, beat down and abandoned by her husband's indifference and Tina's acting out.

The medieval theologian Thomas Aquinas offered a dictum often quoted in Catholic clergy circles: "hurt people hurt people." Aquinas never insisted that such hurt be deliberately malicious. That hurt people hurt people, sometimes deliberately, often accidentally and even mindlessly, was simply a fact of life. No one was immune. Mix that fact of human life into the brew of Dad's hurt, Lil's hurt, and our family hurt, then add in Slovenian rootedness in family and propensity for long hours of storytelling, who knew where the full brew of Dad's dying would lead us.

• • •

The next morning was a Friday, and I had no Mass scheduled. Still, I awoke at five-thirty. I took the dogs out for a walk. I sang the Requiem as we walked, repeating to myself, "My dad is dead. Dad is dead." I found the idea hard to register. I felt no sadness.

When I got back to the rectory, I cut some oranges and prepared the dining room for breakfast while the dogs ate. Then I showered and prayed. Mom and Joe promptly showed for breakfast at eight o'clock.

As we sat and talked, still at table near nine o'clock, the phone rang. It was Jeff Dames.

"Father, I received a call from Lillian this morning. The funeral will be Wednesday at eleven o'clock, with the wake Tuesday afternoon starting at four o'clock. She said that she could not arrange a flight back from Florida so she would stay."

I was surprised, a little miffed that I had not been called, and thought her reasoning, at least as Jeff reported it, off-the-mark. But oh well! She had to make sense of it in her own way so she could live with the decision ever after. I felt delighted by her decision.

Now for step two. "Thank you, Jeff. That will be fine. I would like to talk with you again about cremation. Can we still change that?"

"Yes, Father, there's plenty of time. Of course, Lillian, as legal next-of-kin would have to authorize any change."

"I understand that. Could we make arrangements such that if you received a call from Lillian you could just move right ahead?"

"Yes, Father, that would be fine."

"What precisely would Lillian save if Roger and I paid for the burial?" By habit I wanted all my ducks in a row. This duck, I suspected, would be quite important.

"Lillian would save the cremation fee, the fee for the urn, the vault fee, and the $250 grave opening fee. That would come to near $600."

"Okay. I would like to aim for going ahead with it."

"Do you want the concrete vault or the box?"

"I would like to wait on that question for now. Is that okay?"

"Yes, Father, that's fine." He paused. "Father, what kind of flower arrangement would you like?"

The question ambushed me. I had given flowers no thought. It struck me funny that a mortician's son, who was reminded of a funeral whenever he smells flowers, and a priest who fussed about where funeral flowers were placed in the church, would not think of flowers. "What is Lillian doing, Jeff?"

"She has purchased a large spray of red roses for the casket."

"What is customary for children, sons?"

"Typically, a large spray at the head of the casket."

"What would something like that cost?"

"Between $150 and $200."

Sticker shock! I paused to think it through. Preferring the understated, I thought a spray garish and wasteful. Since the flowers were often taken as an opportunity to say something about love, it occurred to me that I could make a point with the flowers, to Dad and to Lil. Jeff waited patiently. "Jeff, how about two red roses. In the casket with him. No ribbons attached."

"Certainly, Father."

"And two white ones. For his grandchildren."

"That would be fine, Father. Another thing, Father." He was all business. "I spoke with the cemetery. There are only two graves left in the Papesh plot."

"The third grave is that of a child." I instantly remembered.

"Yes. Katerina. You will need to decide who the two graves are for. If your father is buried and Lillian is cremated, then she can be placed in the same grave with him and you can have the other grave. If not, then both graves would be taken. So, a decision needs to be made here."

"Jeff, can I be buried in the Katerina plot?"

"Yes, Father. She was an infant and buried in a wood casket. By now she has gone back to the earth. I have checked with the cemetery and they are willing to let you have that grave."

"What is customary, Jeff? Is that done?" In the past, I had simply thought that I would be buried below Katerina in the same plot. I felt a little uneasy about disturbing the dead, even if she had gone back to the earth.

"You can do as you wish, Father. The cemetery is fine with whatever you wish. However, there is only one stone per plot." I held a vivid memory of a little gray stone with a lamb on top of it marking Katerina's grave. I felt more uneasy. "The decision is yours," he continued.

"Jeff, whatever Lillian wants will be fine. If she dies first and is buried whole, then she can have the grave. If she is cremated, then that's a different matter. I guess we'll just have to wait."

Now seemed the time to settle as much as possible, so I continued. "By the way, Jeff, do folks in Joliet lower during the committal at the cemetery?" We had been doing this at the parish in St. Paul for years, and it was wonderful for the family. The rite was structured for the lowering to occur within it and families uniformly appreciated the sense of completion that came with having the body lowered into the grave while they watched, rather than having the casket hovering suspended over a grave in an open field when they left.

"Yes. We have done that. I can make those arrangements if you wish."

"I would like that. So, now, if you receive a call from Lillian authorizing this, you can just go right ahead?"

"Yes, Father, except for the vault question."

"Excellent. She will likely get back to you. I will, too."

"I am available all morning, Father."

When I got off the phone, Mom and Joe had moved to the living room. My smile told all. Nonetheless, Mom opened with her usual, "Well, what now?"

"One down, one to go. Dad will be waked on Tuesday and the funeral will be Wednesday."

"Oh, that's wonderful!" Mom exclaimed

I then explained to them my conversation with Jeff noting that, once again, Lil had not called. We talked about some of the details.

Then Mom led into a whole new subject. "Joe says that, if you want, I can go down with you and Rog. He can drive back to Colorado and then we'll arrange tickets for me to fly home."

"Wow! I have been thinking about that," I said. Quite a bit, truth told. "If you don't mind, how about both of you coming down? I would like that. It would be wonderfully consoling. And, Joe, I would appreciate having you along very much. It just feels right. Are you okay with that?"

"Yeah, I'm okay with that," Joe said.

"We'll plan on that, then," Mom said. "And, Joe, you can make the reservations for us." She turned to me, saying, "We'll pay for the rooms, too."

"There's no need for you to do that."

"Don't worry, Mike," Joe responded. "Just take care of what you are doing. We'll take care of the rest."

•　　•　　•

After Mom and Joe's marriage, reality set in immediately for Mom. Joe's sixteen-year-old son Mark grated her. Joe's willingness to fight to the death for ten cents on a pint of tomatoes, his stubborn aloofness from helping around the house, his persnickety fussiness about food, and his propagandizing political opinions all surprised Mom. Mom's alienation from home, family and friends, her strained relationship with Roger and me, and our unwillingness to let her help us with our own very messy coming into manhood left Mom feeling isolated.

She found her main support in Grandma Foster. The downside of this was the emotional noise of Mom's having to listen daily to grinding gossip. Mom hated apartment living. Joe's decision to design and build a brand-new home in a new town added further stress.

I left seminary and monastic life in 1975, just after Dad and Lil's marriage, and went to live in Minnesota. Joe's father died in 1976. Roger moved in with Mom and Joe for several months in 1977 and '78. When his work for GTE ended because Roger couldn't handle emotionally the Chicago commute, he insisted on traveling to Florida with a neighboring widow and her two pubescent children. Through Mom, Joe offered Roger a choice. He could stay home and find a new job or go to Florida and move out when he returned.

Roger went to Florida. When he returned, Joe told Rog firmly that he had chosen to move out. Mom played the victim but, if half-heartedly, stuck by Joe's decision. Taken aback, confused, and mad, Roger moved out. Mom, in tears, gave him a tin of cookies as he pulled away in his van.

Roger refused to speak to Mom and Joe afterward but stayed in their new town doing home renovation work among their new friends. Ever the extrovert to Mom and Joe's introversion, and very angry, Roger spread abroad family stories all the while. He finally snuck away to California in the spring of 1979.

In late 1978, Joe was diagnosed with stomach cancer. His stomach was removed and replaced by a small pouch in December of that year. Joe's cancer marked a turning point in our relationships together and changed Mom and Joe's marriage.

It helped everything that Mark, Joe's son, finished college in 1981 and went to work near Denver. Roger began a career at IBM in San

Jose repairing typewriters in late 1979, got married in 1982, and provided the first of two grandchildren, Michael, seven months later. After five years of campus ministry work and extended stays at two monasteries, I went back to seminary in early 1982 and was ordained priest a year later for the Archdiocese of St. Paul and Minneapolis.

During this eventful settling time for us, Joe started seeing life differently. Money, macho, meals, and politics remained a priority, but Joe started setting his sights for retirement in the Rockies. In 1980 he began shopping for property and designing a home at the kitchen table. By 1984, he was offered the choice between a substantial increase of responsibility at "the J" that would have moved him to Pittsburgh, or a parachute. Joe was eager to take the jump. He already owned property in Durango, Colorado and he had already designed the house.

With an eye to the end of their lives, yet still young at fifty-five and fifty-eight, Joe and Mom mellowed during the following years in their acceptance of one another and us. Mom, of course, always worked hard to sustain and deepen relationships with Roger and me. Our settling in, coupled with their own, opened us all to freer and easier relationships. We gathered as family for holidays. Joe's tolerant and Mom's "lace curtain" Irish hospitality felt most gracious. Joe's broad knowledge of finances, real estate, negotiating experience, and administrative expertise drew Roger and I to go to him sometimes with our professional problems. He listened patiently and helped us sort them out. We knew one another's biases and, consequently, where to accept or suspend judgment.

A major milepost of our coming together as a family was my spending a six-month sabbatical in 1998 on Mom and Joe's newly acquired hay ranch near Mesa Verde. We shared stories at meals and hearty laughs over one another's foibles. We grew patient with one another's demands and lapses. Joe's jealousy of my relationship with Mom subsided some, though his pressure to have me do manual labor chores for him continued unabated. We learned some how to argue with each other.

One afternoon during these months, I lost my four-month old boxer puppy in the hay field. Joe, deeply sentimental about animals, felt angry but hid it even when a car ride turned up nothing. I continued the search after the ride, finding the puppy on the main road a short while later.

As I walked into the inner yard with the newfound puppy, from the back-porch Joe yelled, "That dog should always be on a leash. He could have been killed. Well, have you finally learned your lesson?"

Not one to be dominated, I responded, "Yeah, for today I suppose. But who knows what tomorrow will bring?"

"You are a damned, stubborn roundhead, you are!" He was still emotional.

"W-e-e-ll, that from a Chicago Pollack!" I blurted back.

Joe prided himself on his Italian heritage because he so loved his easy-going father. A thoroughbred Chicago Pole, his mother was a fussy perfectionist and domineering over her only child. Though he denied it, Joe was more his mother's than his father's son.

"I'd rather be that than a damned roundhead!" He walked in the house.

Furious, I walked into the house after him and popped off in the kitchen, saying, "He's my dog. While I appreciate your care about him, he is my dog. What I do with him is none of your business." I walked upstairs. Mom likely got an earful in the kitchen.

After calming down, then torturing myself alone in my room over the exchange, I went downstairs a couple of hours later and caught Joe in his den. "I am sorry, Joe," I said. "I got carried away. I really do appreciate your concern, and I know you are right about the leash."

"Well thanks, Mike. I just wouldn't want to see anything happen to him."

This kind of event, several times over, drew us gradually to engage each other somewhat as persons, though we remained essentially joined less with each other than in relationship to and through Mom.

We gradually, if bumpily, became like family; Mom and Joe with each other, they with Roger and me, and us with them. That sense emerged out of traumatic emotional confusion, Joe's pursuit of relationship in a way that would today open him to prosecution for sexual harassment, and the excruciating pain of divorce. What we achieved remained abidingly tenuous and fragile, but nonetheless helpful, especially for Mom.

CHAPTER III
Re-Arrangements 2: Burying Dad Whole

Since I had to go to the parish office, I left Mom and Joe in the living room. The office was quiet. People kindly and gently extended their sympathies as I walked through. I had two calls on my voicemail. One came from Lil at 7:00 A.M. telling me the funeral would be Wednesday. The other was from O'Halloran and Murphy Funeral Home in St. Paul. I returned their call and was forwarded to one of the members of the embalming staff.

"Father, people have been calling us about your father's death. What address should I give them for flowers?"

"Really, Tom? Wow! How about if they not give flowers and just send memorials to the Holy Spirit Building Fund. We'll figure out precisely what to do with the money later."

"Okay, Father. That will work. My sympathies to you from one funeral director to another."

"Thanks, Tom."

I shared with Mary, the Principal, and Mary, the Business Administrator, some of the accumulating family stories. I let the front desk at the parish know about memorials. Then I decided to call St. Joe's in Joliet. I asked for Fr. George Klepec, who, like me, had been raised in the parish. He was unavailable. I told the secretary I would like to see Fr. George sometime next Tuesday to go over the ceremony plans. She set the time for a quarter after nine, after his morning Mass.

As I walked out of the office, Mary, the Principal, caught me. "Are you going to be around for a few minutes? A couple of middle school students would like to see you."

I felt anxiety surge. "Yes, but I'll be here only briefly."

Mary saw the anxiety in my face. "Okay. I will get them right away."

I walked into the commons, where a mural was in progress. I wanted to see how far the artist had gotten on the mural before his equipment had to be removed. At sixteen by fifty-two feet, the massive work demanded a focus Richard truly struggled to give it, and he felt justifiably proud. He had not gotten far enough as I saw it, but I simply needed to let that go. His teasing me about my being Julius II to his Michelangelo had hit its mark. The two-story, arched hall looked better clear, though.

When I turned the corner around the office reception desk, Mary stood at attention. "The students are here," she said.

I walked into the little conference room next to her office and there sat two seventh grade boys, Joe and Ian. I settled between them at the round table.

"Father," Ian began, "the middle school took up a collection for a tree for your father. So, we would like to give you this card and check for the tree."

They handed me a card with one hundred signatures on it and a check. My eyes immediately welled with tears. The parish had been collecting funds for fifty-five new trees, and we were asking a brisk $300 apiece. There it was.

"I don't know what to say! Thank you very much. I am really touched that you would all be so thoughtful and so generous. I am very grateful, and my family will be, too."

They certainly didn't know how to handle my tears, or what to say. They immediately stood up. "Well, we are praying for your father, Father."

"Thank you, Joe and Ian. Please give my thanks to everyone."

The boys left. Mary stood outside her office.

"I am amazed at this," I said to her, showing her the card.

"It was their idea," she said. "They wanted to do something. Even though the eighth graders have been gone for three days, they pulled it all together."

"Well thanks, Mary. Wow!"

Feeling a little shaky, I took the card and gift three doors down to my office, then decided to head back to the rectory.

Joe had already taken the dogs out. Mom, putzing around the kitchen, wanted to hear all about what had transpired during the morning thus far. We went into the living room and the three of us sat down. Mom and Joe, too, felt amazed at the children's' kindness – not to mention their parents' kindness.

But I had business to attend to in Illinois. "Well, it's time to call Lil again. Here goes round two."

"Mike, it's a shame that you have to go through all this," Mom said.

Joe had a look of worldly-wise wonderment on his face, but said, "Go for it!"

"Just pray that this goes well. It's the tough one." I headed upstairs.

•　　　•　　　•

Devastated by divorce from Mom, Dad had sought emotional support from Roger and me. Roger, always inclined to keep things light and moving, full of restless energy and bold stories, provided Dad distraction and companionship. One evening, shooting the breeze with a Roger and a friend, Dad even tried marijuana. Roger's outrageous behavior gave strait-laced Dad a lift.

At the time, I resided at a Southern Indiana monastery. In early July, Dad and Roger came down for a weekend visit. We talked about what had happened and Dad's resolve to pull back from work. He evidently thought that his priority on work cost him his marriage. It did, but Dad's analysis was partial.

On Sunday morning, as I was out for a walk in the monastery garden, I found Dad in tears. I had never seen him cry, and he immediately stopped when he saw me. He told me he didn't know what to do with himself. He wanted Mom back. Roger appeared from the Guest House and the conversation ended.

A month later, on August 6, I visited home for the first time since entering the monastery two years before. Because the day of my arrival was also Grandma Foster's birthday, Roger and I stopped by to see her. The mission was to let her see me for the first time in two years and wish her happy birthday without getting into anything that had happened over the past months. We feared our time together might degenerate into hurling accusations. Our mission accomplished in less than an hour, Roger and I returned home and joined Dad on the backyard patio.

Dad knew I most likely had a fuller sense than Roger of what was going on with Mom. Open and vulnerable, he let out his longing. "Mike, I want to get your mom back. Please let her know that I am always open if she would be willing to take me back. Would you do that for me?"

I froze. I looked at Roger and he at me. He froze, too. "Dad," I said, "Mom married four days ago."

Dad froze. He then put his right hand to his chin, with his index finger curved across his lips. Everything about his posture spoke complete emotional withdrawal. "Oh. Okay, Son," he said slowly.

"I'm sorry. I thought you knew."

"That's okay, Son." The conversation over, we dispersed into the house.

•   •   •

Mickey Papesh and Mary Jean Beaudry began seeing one another on-and-off at the neighborhood gathering place, the Hickory Street School playground, during 1939. The apartment Mom moved into that year with Grandma, Grandma's second husband, Art, and Mom's sister, Joanie, sat only three blocks from the Papesh homestead. Mickey and Mary Jean remembered each other from his playing the saxophone and her playing the clarinet in the band at St. Joe's in 1936, but their connection back then had been light. Mickey was seven months older than Mary Jean; he was a grade behind her. She had skipped a grade while he had started school late.

Dad and Mom kissed for the first time that same year at the back of Trobe's, a neighborhood grocery store. A group of friends hung around there and occasionally played "post office." When alone the first time, Mickey and Mary Jean agreed not to kiss. The second time Dad and Mom sat at bottle-point, they kissed. Mickey began penetrating Mary Jean's shy reserve in 1940 when he entered high school and the two walked down Broadway together to school. Mickey and Mary Jean's relationship began growing closer when Dad started biking up to the Summit St. apartment after school and calling for Mom. They would sit out front on the porch steps and talk for an hour until Grandpa Papesh came by at four o'clock to pick up Dad for work at the tavern. They also got to know one another better through school socials and roller-skating parties.

In high school, Mom liked another boy, Jake Bebar. Dad had been going with Lillian Kobe since grade school. He had gifted Lil through the years with pins he kept on his beanie. In the spring of 1941, Dad told Mom that he liked her better than Lillian Kobe and had decided to ask Lil for all his pins back, which he did. All three of them understood that to be a serious step in their relationship.

•　　•　　•

When Dad first confided to Grandma Papesh about Mom's relationship with Joe, Grandma immediately let it be known that Lil was available because she was to be divorced in July. Though Lil "had a reputation around town," Grandma nonetheless approved of Lil for sentimental reasons and because she was Slovenian, like the Papeshes.

At one point in March 1974, Dad taunted Mom with Grandma's remark about Lil, saying, "Mom says Lillian Kobe is available." A shy but jealous truce had long existed between Mom and Lil.

"That's fine with me," Mom snapped back to Dad. "You can have her."

Dad later told Roger and me that he ran into Lil in downtown Joliet on August 13, a week after I left home to go back to the monastery. Years later, Lil told me that Dad confessed that he had planned their meeting by waiting in Jehle's Jewelers, across the street from the bank where Lil worked, until, at lunchtime, Lil came out of the bank. They went on their first date on August 19, 1974. They married sixteen months later.

Dad confided to me that he found their early dating relationship difficult. He felt trembling nervous, emotionally tender, and disliked even being touched. As time passed, his ease and enthusiasm increased. Viewing Mom as reserved sexually, about three months into their dating relationship Dad expressed delight in Lil's pleasure in sex. "We can do it any way you want," she had told him. Dad liked that.

I met Lil in November 1974 when Dad, Grandma Papesh, Gloria, and Lil drove down to the monastery for a visit. I was angry and confused that he was already determined that I needed to meet her and approve so he might remarry.

The family stayed in an old but renovated two-bedroom home on monastery property that had formerly been used by lay workers. As I entered the house to welcome them, Lil stood outside a bathroom wearing a robe. She was drawing a bath. She struck me from a distance as Mom with red hair. Explaining that we could not get together right away because Lil felt nervous about bathing in a strange place and he was trying to make her comfortable, Dad assured me the two of them would be along soon. I walked upstairs to see Grandma and Gloria.

Grandma Papesh and Gloria sat together in the upstairs bedroom, each on the end of a twin bed. I greeted them and sat down on a nearby chair.

"Did you meet Lil?" Gloria asked with a telling look in her eye.

"I only saw her. She's evidently nervous about taking a bath. Dad is helping her."

"You'll like her," Grandma said gushing. "And your dad is so happy."

"But she is not my mother!" I snapped angrily.

They both immediately broke into tears.

The visit got more comfortable, though it remained cool. By its end I could tell that marriage was inevitable. Though she had known Dad well in the years when everyone called Dad "Mickey," Lil was now calling Dad "Michael." Dad called Lil by pet names he had used for Mom. What I heard and saw chafed.

After they married in their living room before a justice of the peace on St. Nicholas Day – a Saturday morning in 1975 – Dad and Lil settled into the same patterns Dad had maintained with Mom, with two glaring exceptions. He gave his relationship with Lil priority over work. And going out drinking and dancing with friends became their main free time activity.

Dad called Lil his "buddy," spoke often about being out with people at clubs and bars, and typically remarked, as if it were funny, "Aw-haw-haw! Did we tie one on!" or "Did I have one hell of a hangover the next morning! Awwwww!" Dad's life centered on Lil and conformed to whatever were her interests. With different priorities – work, then sex, but markedly stay-at-home socially – I had witnessed the same behavior toward Mom when I was living at home. Though I felt turned off by Dad and Lil's drinking especially, I diligently worked internally to let go and let be.

I left monastic life around the time of Dad and Lil's marriage and moved to Minnesota. Preoccupied with putting a new life together and making sense of it, I remained confusedly ambivalent about Dad and Lil and how they passed their time. I called about once a month, forwarded an occasional note, sent birthday cards, and gave fussy bauble gifts at Christmas. I visited at least once a year, twice a year when they lived in Illinois. I did my duty toward them for Dad's sake but remained pleasantly reserved when I visited them. We all treaded lightly.

Roger's relationship with them was freer. While I knew he shared some of my confused ambivalence, Rog loved to party and continued to be "a character" with them. The turmoil of Rog's life entertained Dad and Lil, but they carefully kept a reserved emotional distance from Roger's confusion. When Rog lived in Illinois, Dad and Lil discouraged him from living at home and Dad remained keen that Roger respect Lil's privacy in the bedroom or bathroom when he stayed overnight with them. At the same time, Dad and Lil regaled at Roger's colorful stories and shared them freely. This ambivalence in relationship kept Roger away, which was likely what Dad preferred. Roger's stories, however zany, never seemed to worry Dad and Lil or suggest they felt genuinely concerned about Roger. They treated him and talked about him as if he were a comedy sideshow.

In the summer of 1978, I went home to Joliet for a couple of weeks to visit with the family. I had just completed a master's degree, felt proud of myself, and had presented a copy of the thesis to Mom and Joe and one to Dad and Lil.

One evening, after Lil had gone to bed, Dad uncharacteristically lingered. He came to me at the television room doorway holding the thesis in his right hand.

"Mike, I can't keep this. I read up to the acknowledgments. I stopped where you thank your mother and Joe for their hospitality while you wrote it, talking about 'their beautiful home.' I can't keep it in this house. Who can I show it to? So, here, you can have it back." He calmly, delicately handed me the thesis.

"Oh! Okay, Dad." My whole body was hot with anger as I took the thesis from him. He turned and went to his bedroom.

I watched TV absently, stewing. I felt insulted, angry at his touchiness, angrier still that he was neither man, nor father enough to rise above my genuine expression of gratitude to Mom and Joe. I sat wordlessly mulling for a long time. Then, thesis in hand, I went to their ajar bedroom door, knocked, and opened the door into the darkness.

"Dad."

"Huh? What is it, Son?"

"Michael?" Lil said. They had both been asleep.

"Dad, I am giving this thesis back to you. You can do what you want with it. Throw it away. Burn it. Tear it into a thousand pieces. Do whatever you want with it. But I gave it to you. I am not taking it out of this house. It's yours. The ball is in your court." Unwaveringly firm, this act was a first for me with Dad.

"Oh! Okay, Son," he said.

I put the thesis on their dresser and walked out. Other than my hearing their muffled talk immediately afterward, I never heard anything more. I never saw the thesis again, either.

I went out with Dad and Lil only once, a Saturday night in September 1978. My cousin John Michael, Gloria's eldest, had gotten married earlier in the day and the reception ended about nine o'clock. To my surprise, Aunt Gloria, Uncle John, Dad, and Lil wanted to go out for a while. I agreed, and we all went to a bar for some talk and dancing.

Dad and Lil each sipped two drinks to my one. I also beheld Lil passively receive the mauling attentions of a male acquaintance. I felt like squirming, uncomfortable with what I saw and irritable about it.

As we were rising to head out, Lil fell off a barstool onto the floor. She seemed to feel mortified. We all passed it off in the moment as if it were nothing. Dad thought it funny.

In the car, Dad, Lil, and I sat across the front seat, Lil in the middle. Evidently still mortified, she remarked, "Oh, Michael, whatever will you think of me after falling on the floor like that?"

Embarrassed by her behavior, realizing in that moment that I resented their lifestyle and Dad's laughing about the fall, I overreacted. "I have never known Mrs. Michael Papesh to behave like that in public."

Silence thundered during the ride home.

Though I later thought my response pompous, arrogant, and stupid, I never talked with Lil or Dad about it and never apologized. By the time my fault registered, I was unsure how to apologize, or if an apology might make things worse. Yet from that point forward, Lil's and my relationship stood still. Hyper-protective of Lil, Dad probably felt miffed. At the same time, because of his own habitual public reserve over many years, I knew Dad understood.

Later in 1978, Dad and Lil moved to Florida. They billed the move as retirement. In fact, Dad had issued his employer, Mark Dames, an ultimatum. As manager of Fred C. Dames Funeral Home and a partner for three percent of his own annual business there, Dad told Mark that he wanted a salary increase by a set date, or he would leave. The date passed with nothing said.

Having badly miscalculated, feeling disillusioned and far too proud to back down, Dad determined to leave Dames Funeral Home. Several weeks later, when Mark offered Dad the raise he asked, it was too late. Moving to Florida was the only way Dad could see to keep his dignity.

Though I had received no Christmas card or gift, and had no idea what to make of that, I visited them in Florida in January 1979. His whole life, Dad had spent what he earned. At fifty-four, he had no retirement but Social Security. Needing to save face in front of the Joliet Slovenian community about his retirement, yet still having to work, Dad sought jobs in Florida having nothing to do with funeral directing. He held about nineteen of them during a three-year period before he finally went back to funeral directing. That January, Dad was holding his second Florida job, this one selling furniture. Lil was in sales at a small retail uniforms shop. They put on a happy face, but times were tough.

One evening we sat around the living room talking. As I sipped some wine, Dad and Lil had a couple of Manhattans. Dad, it turned out, was fortifying himself.

"I have a couple of bones to pick with you, Son," he began. Then he was off! He told me that he had worked hard to provide for Roger and me and he deserved better than he was getting from us. As he catalogued all he had done, I could not help but agree. He was a hard worker and had been so all his life. Though I was unsure that his work was done for us, he had provided generously. We lacked nothing. Indeed, for years we thought we were rich.

As I listened, I began to realize that Dad and I meant different things by the word *love*. I believed love meant spending time, sharing thoughts and feelings, and enjoying one another's company. Rarely around for that kind of love, Dad seemed not to care that we talked only superficially or evasively about what one another thought or felt. For Dad, *love* apparently meant "doing" for someone. If we did for each other, then we loved, he seemed to assume. I had never thought of love that way, at least in stark terms, and certainly never knew Dad did. He clearly believed he loved, and I failed to love in return. I, on the other hand, had lived my whole life with the anxious suspicion that Dad failed to love, at least meaningfully. Our different understandings stood out starkly in the conversation. With his anger barking and scratching at the door, however, Dad and I exploring the meaning of love was out of the question. Nonetheless, I could certainly agree that Dad had worked hard, very hard. "I know, Dad. I appreciate all you have done for us," was all I could muster.

He went on. "I am sick and tired of writing a ghost in Minnesota. If you called here and I left the phone hanging on the floor for twenty-four hours, you owe me that for all I have done for you."

Dad had sent me typed letters a couple of times a month for eight years while I was away. I responded to a few, called home shortly after some, but I wrote irregularly and never addressed his content. His letters were chatty, usually one-page pieces done at the office when he had free time. Preoccupied by intense and confusing emotions across my life, I was impatient with chattiness. My skill at it had always been nil. Dad's letters seemed mundane, and his people references unknown to me mostly, so I tended to dismiss his letters. After he and Lil married, I felt justified about my lackadaisical attitude since I not only personally knew few of the people he referred to, I was also ill-at-ease about the social life he reported. Still, sitting in the heat of that moment, I thought I probably should write more.

He called rarely, but I still felt ashamed I did not call him more. I agreed with him that I ought to change. "I know, Dad," I eventually said. "I should try to do better. I am sorry about that."

Though I was unsure precisely where the border was between what was really Dad and what was the Manhattans, Dad evidently grew increasingly confident. He was "on a roll," as he would say. Attentive, I felt embarrassed and chastened. Lil sat silently sipping. She seemed uncomfortable.

After supplementing his main points with sundry illustrations, he said with meaning, "I feel as if I have paid for two Rolls Royces and I have yet to see a Model A in the driveway."

Whatever shame I felt instantly vanished. My eyes flashed. Fire ran down my body. His calling Roger and I failures outraged me. I had seven years more education than Dad and two degrees to show for it. I was the youngest Catholic university director of campus ministry in the country, and one of only two laymen in the position nationally. Roger's life was a mess presently, but I felt confident he would be fine. He had a four-year college degree and worked hard. Dad either didn't get all that or chose not to. I also surged indignant at the implication that because he had paid, we owed him love. I was willing to try friendship with him if he was willing. Duty I could also do, even if I wasn't sure if

I wanted that kind of relationship with him. Homage, however, I would never give. I glared at him, furious.

Dad immediately understood he had gone too far. He started shifting in his chair, looking into his drink. Lil, alert, looked back and forth between us. Wide-eyed, flushed behind a new sunburn, I sat stone silent, ready to remain so for eternity.

Dad, eyes downcast, rose and went into the kitchen to refresh his drink. He came back and moved the conversation onto other things. I calmed as he chatted about who-knows-what. A bathroom break and bed shortly afterward ended our time together.

Throughout my life, I never felt that Dad made the effort to understand my life or me. I right then knew that understanding was beyond him. Lil stood as witness. Understanding may well have been beyond her, too.

At the end of the Florida visit, in the airport, Dad slipped me a twenty-dollar bill "for Christmas." The gesture felt flaccid.

In the years after, I maintained the same stuttering pattern of calls, letter writing, birthday cards, and Christmas gifts. Dad wrote less and less, leaving it to me, until his writing stopped altogether. He never again called. I received a birthday card and a Christmas card, rarely a gift.

I approached my communication with him as doing my duty, and I determined to hang-in with my duty no matter what. Dad likely expected something more or other, but I could only guess at what he thought. We never discussed the January 1979 exchange.

I exposed a glimmer of what I thought about Dad's situation three years later. In early August 1982, I received a call at the seminary from Mom that Roger was getting married. Roger had spoken to us about his wanting to marry a girl eleven years his junior. He even gave us a wedding date at one point. Messages, though, were mixed. She wanted to marry, he said, but was too shy to go through a ceremony. They set a date, then canceled it because of her shyness. That was the story. We simply waited to see what would happen. Roger now reported to Mom that the girl was pregnant, and due in March. Roger planned to get married.

Not knowing what to make of things, I asked Mom what she thought about it. She said she told Rog she was sorry he was getting married under these circumstances. He didn't have to do this if he really didn't want to. However, she would support him in whatever he chose to do.

When I asked if she pressed him, she was emphatic that she didn't want to threaten their relationship in any way after years of walking on eggshells with him. I understood that.

I called Dad to ask if he had heard. He had. When I asked what he thought, he said, "Whatever he wants, Son."

I received that response as code for what I experienced as Dad's monumental indifference to our choices throughout our lives. Whatever he may have meant by it, when I heard that phrase, I took it to mean that he didn't care. Roger was his favorite. His not caring was incomprehensible. I felt angry but said nothing.

In a fit of "big brother fever" I called Roger. Roger gloated that Karen had gotten pregnant on the very day they had originally scheduled for their marriage. He was planning to marry her in Reno. Roger sounded self-satisfied, devil-may-care, braggadocious – as if a twenty-nine-year-old man desperate to marry had just trapped an eighteen-year-old into it. I thought that a recipe for failure.

"Roger, you don't have to marry her. There are other options." I was intent that Roger get this point since our parents, in my view, had not fulfilled their responsibility to him, Mom out of fear, Dad out of indifference.

"Like what, Mike?"

"You could wait. Karen could have the baby, then you could take some time to see if marrying her is what you really want. Pregnancy creates tension and pressure. It is not necessarily the best time to make a life decision. It might help to wait until after the baby is born, then decide."

"Mike, I want to get married."

I persisted. "Rog, you could also have the child adopted."

"Mike," he said heatedly, "I am getting married and I don't give a damn what you think about it." I had pushed him to the limit. Enough.

"I just wanted you to know that there are other options," I told him.

The next day, worried, self-righteous, and mad about what I saw as Dad's cavalier, don't care attitude toward his favorite son during the messiness of this momentous life decision, I decided to write him. In the letter – one page, single-spaced – I told him I thought he had abdicated his responsibility toward Roger. I made it clear that I thought his drinking and going from job to job in Florida these years had dulled him to his real responsibilities toward us, especially in situations like this. I told him he ought to care.

One week later I got an oversized envelope from him. Inside sat my letter to Dad in its envelope, open, but without comment. It felt like a thunderclap of indignation. Unwittingly, I had accused Lil, too, of not caring for us.

●　　●　　●

When I got to my rectory bedroom, I called Lynn and she put Lil on the line.

"Hi, Lil. I got a message from Jeff Dames this morning. Thank you for being willing to rearrange the time for the funeral."

"Oh, that's okay. I couldn't get the flights to work out so I thought I might as well stay. Besides, I need the rest very badly. I have asked a neighbor to get Dad's clothes and to send up one of my dresses. I really didn't have anything to wear here. So, it looks like everything will work out. I have arranged with Jeff to see Dad Tuesday morning so we can have some time."

"Great. I am glad things are happening this way. It works out well for us, and I think you will be in a better place when the wake begins."

"Yeah, I think so, too."

"Lil, there's one more thing."

"Yes?" Instantly, her voice sounded more tentative.

"I am wondering if you would consider not cremating Dad but burying him whole. Roger and I would be happy to pay the difference."

"I have just gotten everything arranged and now you want to mess it up again?" She was angry.

"Lil, Rog and I feel uncomfortable about the cremation."

"It was his wishes to be cremated. Why would you want to go against his wishes?" She sounded vehement, but I knew too much to be stopped by that.

"Lil, Dad never spoke to me or to Roger that cremation would be his wishes. We would like to bury him whole."

"I knew you and Roger would not like cremation," she spat.

I felt mystified. Had she hoped to avoid controversy by making all the decisions without us? Was this Dad's old to-hell-with-them attitude?

"Yes, Lil, we prefer to have Dad buried whole. Roger and I would be happy to pay the difference. I have spoken with Jeff Dames and you wouldn't have to worry about a thing. All you need do is give the word. Everything is all set."

"You mean you changed my arrangements!"

"No, Lil. The arrangements are still the ones you made. What you want is what we will do."

"Well, that's better."

I immediately grasped that power was more of an issue for Lil than I knew. "I have talked it through completely with Jeff Dames," I went on. "If you would be willing to let Dad be buried whole, all Jeff needs is for you to call and authorize that. He will take things from there. The only thing you need to do is make a phone call. Otherwise things stay as they are now."

"I have to think about this. I need some time."

"That's fine, Lil. I appreciate your willingness to even consider it.

Roger and I would be happy to do it."

"I will call you back in a half hour or so." She was calming down.

"That would be great. By the way, I have called Fr. George and I will get together with him to plan the funeral on Tuesday morning. Is there any music you would especially like to hear?"

"Yes. I would like the *Ave Maria* and the *Cecenye Maria*, I think it's called. It's an old Slovenian hymn."

Dad had no special devotion to the Blessed Virgin that I knew about. Though the *Ave Maria* was a war-horse of a tune for funerals, I wasn't sure why it was appropriate for Dad. I liked the idea of a Slovenian song for him, no matter the words. But the important thing right now was to keep peace at most any price. "Okay, that would be fine. How about *On Eagles' Wings*?"

That, too, was a war-horse hymn for funerals and it was becoming indispensable. I thought she would like it.

"That would be fine." It didn't matter to her.

"I have nothing else to suggest, Lil. Unless you want something in particular, I thought I would just let the parish do what the parish does. That would probably work best."

"That's okay with me." Nope, it didn't matter.

My Irish heritage suddenly kicked in. I knew it would cost Roger and me. I also thought the appeal a little low. Yet I decided in an instant that it was worth it. "Oh, by the way, Lil, if you decide to have Dad buried whole, you would save nearly $600. You wouldn't have to pay for the cremation, the urn, the urn vault, or the grave opening. We would take care of everything after the church."

"Oh, okay," she said quickly. She seemed to have perked up. I had struck just the right note.

"Well, thanks, Lil. I'll be in touch."

"Goodbye, Michael." Chilly, but we made it.

When I went downstairs, Mom and Joe still sat in the living room. I told the story. Mom especially appreciated that my Irish kicked in. "Mike, I think you've done it. How could she possibly refuse if it saves her $600? She knows your father would never want to be cremated anyway. She and Mark Dames cooked that up just to save money."

"Good job, Mike," Joe joined in. "You're doing the right thing."

Joe then excused himself to go straighten out things in the car before lunch. When he left, Mom turned to me. "Mike, Joe says that he will give you $1,000 toward the burial."

"What? Really?" Generosity was Joe's weak suit; he rarely played it.

"Yeah," she said quite happily. "He brought it up. I didn't say anything about it. He thinks you and Roger are doing the right thing and he wants to help."

I felt deeply touched, even teary. "Mom, that's utterly unnecessary. Amazing, but utterly unnecessary."

"No, he wants to do it, so let it happen." She was happy about it, and definitive.

"Wow!" I went upstairs with my mind racing.

Joe had a ham sandwich with piccalilli and a bowl of soup for lunch. Mom and I each ate a liver sausage sandwich and skipped the soup.

The phone rang. "Well, here's the answer," I said out loud. I ran to the front in-house office. It was Jeff Dames.

"Father, I just spoke with Lillian. She has given permission to have your father buried at St. Joe's."

"Wonderful, Jeff. Wonderful."

"I will go ahead and make the arrangements, then. The casket is here. I will notify the cemetery. Oh, Father, what about the concrete box versus the vault?"

"I am not sure yet, Jeff. I will call you back on that. Do we have time?"

"Yes, Father, that would be fine."

"Also, Father, if your stepmother asks about the cost of the casket, what do you want me to tell her?"

"Will there be one bill?"

"I can separate the bills, Father. That would be no problem."

"Please separate the bills, then, Jeff. But if she asks, feel free to tell Lillian the cost. If she doesn't ask, don't volunteer it."

"Fine, Father. Please let me know about the vault soon."

"I'll get back to you, Jeff. My brother comes in this afternoon." I went back to lunch with the news. Mom was thrilled with my report.

"Well, congratulations, Mike. Things are going to happen like they should," was Mom's delighted response.

"Good work, Mike," Joe piped in.

"Thank you both," I said with a smile. "At least now we can do right by Dad."

"By the way, Mike," Joe began. "I would like to give you $1,000 toward the bill. $3,335 is it?"

I could feel myself getting all wobbly inside again. "You don't have to do that, Joe." That was a courtesy line I was long ago taught to extend.

"I want to. You are going through lots to do the right thing and I want to help. And now you can get the vault."

I felt tears well up. "Well, thank you. I hardly know what to say. I appreciate it very much."

"I'll take care of making the motel arrangements in Joliet and I will pick that up, too. You and Rog shouldn't have to worry about that."

"Wow! Joe, I am overwhelmed. I don't know what to say."

"Don't worry about it. I am glad to do it."

"Thank you," was all I could think to say. For her part, Mom was all smiles.

"Well, excuse me. I have to make a couple of phone calls." I went to the rectory office.

I called Jeff back to let him know about the vault. He said he would take care of everything.

"Jeff, when does the family need to be there for the wake?"

"At three-thirty, Father. Lillian will be coming in that morning to see him in private."

"Jeff, would it be possible for my brother and I to have a private viewing as well? It would be very helpful for us to have that before we get together with the family." I was thinking that Mom and Joe might join in, too. The rest of the family would not be thrilled if they even found out about that, much less have Mom and Joe walk into the wake.

"That would be fine, Father. Any time after one o'clock."

"Oh, Jeff, one more thing. Could you have a little brass band at either the church on the way out, or at the cemetery?"

"We do lots of different things, Father – harps, flute, oboe – but this is the first time anyone has asked for a brass band."

"Just a few pieces, three or four, would be fine. Do you think you could do it?"

"I'll try, Father."

"Thank you. I appreciate that." I decided that I would keep the information about the brass band to myself. I was unsure it would be appreciated, by Mom especially.

•   •   •

Michael Leopold Papesh was named after both of his grandfathers. He was born November 3, 1925, fourteen months after the wedding of Michael Martin Papesh, Jr. and his grocery market employee, Anna Dorothy Vesel. His parents invariably called him Mickey to distinguish him from his father and grandfather. He was their first child. His father, who owned the first grocery store in Joliet to make home delivery, had put a fancy new buggy in the store window months before Mickey's birth. A raging extrovert with the sensibilities of a showman, his father had his wife and the baby met by a brass band at the door of old St. Joseph's Hospital on Broadway the day they were released after Mickey's birth.

• • •

"Is there anything else, Father?"

"No. Thank you, Jeff. You have been just wonderful about everything so far."

"Father, I hear that phrase 'so far' in there." He clearly expected to perform perfectly for us as a family.

"Well, Jeff, this is family. Who knows how things will end up!"

CHAPTER IV
Embracing Reality: Son, Not Preacher

Roger's plane was due at three o'clock. Mom decided to go along for the ride to the airport. Joe stayed at the rectory to watch a ball game. I shared with Mom on the way my pleasure at making the arrangement changes, my gratitude to God that we were all together, and my wonderment that I had yet to feel any sadness about Dad's death. We chatted lightly until I turned the car over to her and went into the terminal to get Roger. Because the plane was late, its arrival time having changed twice, I hung around in the terminal while Mom, afraid she would run out of gas and concerned about burning the pork tenderloin in the rectory oven, rode round and round outside. I left the terminal for the turnabout once to touch base with her. For all her anxiety about gas and the roast, time was on her side.

When Roger got off the plane, I greeted him with the usual hug and, as we walked through the terminal to baggage claim, I filled him in on the results of my discussions with Lil and with Jeff Dames. He thought the re-arrangements the only sensible course. "Oh, good! I don't know what in the hell was going on with Lil," he quipped.

"Now you can arrange your flight to go out of O'Hare," I suggested.

"No problem! That will be easy compared to what was going to happen. That was nuts."

"And guess what, Rog? Joe is going to give us $1,000 toward the casket."

"What?" Roger seemed as struck as I had been.

"Yeah, he wants to help us out and give us a thousand."

"That's wonderful. Dad wouldn't like it," he said with a smirk, eyes bright, shoulders and hands raised in a happy shrug. "But, hey, he's not here to complain!" Roger's humor typically followed the direction of a matter-of-fact coalescing of incongruent facts, or the outrageous exaggeration of them. His bluntness, coupled with utter disregard for the limits of propriety in any company, could be hilarious.

"Hey, Rog, I have got to tell you something I thought very strange. When I was talking with Jeff Dames, he told me that Dad was the only employee they ever had that they trusted to be alone in the building. Isn't that weird, especially for a manager of the place?"

"O-o-o-o-o-oh yeah! Very strange. And Dad thought he was really something at Dames'." Rog, too, thought the remark demeaned Dad.

Mom saw us on the turnabout and veered to the curb. I took over the driver's seat again as Mom and Rog greeted one another and we headed for the rectory. The two of them, very much alike, chatted lightly and quickly about his flights, about what he thought of Lil's original arrangements and the subsequent changes, and about Michael. The fifteen minutes to the rectory were jammed tight. When we got in, I took Roger to his room on the first floor and Joe came down from the TV room to greet him. The phone rang, so I excused myself.

"Michael, this is John." It was Gloria's eldest, John Michael. Named for his father and our grandfather, he was the third Papesh grandchild, a year younger than Roger. The family called him by both his names when he was little both to distinguish him from his father and to emphasize that he was a Papesh, too. Though it had toned down more recently, a tinge of jealously was part of life between Dad and Gloria for many years. Johnny's appellation said so.

"I just wanted to call to say that if there's anything I can do to help, I would be glad to," John said. "If you need money or anything, just ask."

Though I thought it condescending and mildly braggadocious for John to offer money – spillage from Gloria and Dad's jealous relationship I suspected – I decided he intended his offer to be kind and utterly sincere. John did well financially, selling mortgage loans and driving trucks. A true Papesh, he worked very hard. He supported four children by his first wife and lived comfortably with his second. However, my Irish did rear its head again; I wouldn't dream of asking John for money to bury my father. Besides, if he did, the Farkases would crow about it for the rest of their lives. Perhaps there was another contribution he could make. Could he read the Scriptures at the funeral Mass? Probably not. Other things?

"Thanks, John. I appreciate that very much. I am not sure what you might do. It does occur to me, though, that we will probably be needing pallbearers. You would have to talk with Lil about that, but I am sure Dad would like that."

John Michael had been a favorite of Dad's for a couple of decades. Johnny looked up to Uncle Mick. His enthusiasm while in Dad's company, even visiting him in Florida once, and the sparkle in his eyes, let Dad know that. Dad responded to his admiration. I came to know how completely at Dad's seventieth birthday party.

•   •   •

Roger and I instigated with Lil the celebration of Dad's seventieth birthday. His Alzheimer's disease, diagnosed a year earlier, left us probably short on time with Dad, and we assumed it would not be much. The Alzheimer's kept him from driving and making sense of a dashboard or calendar, but otherwise Dad remained in excellent health. We decided that his seventieth birthday was the time to do something special for him. It was, perhaps, our only shot at it.

Roger and I flew into Sarasota the evening of November 2, rented a car, then spent the night in a hotel near Dad and Lil's because Roger had gotten in far too late for us to make a civil appearance. We went to Dad and Lil's home shortly after breakfast, singing happy birthday when he opened the door. It was a surprise. Dad, pleased to see us, greeted us with his characteristic, "We-e-e-e-ll, hello there! How are you?"

We hugged him and went to the kitchen table to talk. Dad was all smiles. Gloria came later that day. Her arrival was, by then, expected. John Michael planned to come from Texas, where he was then living with his new wife, but nothing had been said to Dad about Johnny's coming.

Late in the afternoon, we went to the hotel for the guests' assembly. Lil scheduled the event in the back room of a restaurant: white walls, captain's chairs, a small private bar. The dining room was adjacent, comfortable for about twelve. Mark and Sharon Dames came, as did a woman friend of Lil's and Lil's daughter Tina.

Roger and I were standing near the bar talking with Mark and Sharon Dames when John Michael and his wife arrived through double doors on our right. Dad was on our left down the room some talking with Lil and her friend. Dad looked at Johnny coming through the door and immediately broke into tears. Johnny looked at Dad and, completely ill-at-ease with the display of emotion, awkwardly entered the room and greeted Aunt Gloria.

Roger stepped forward to say hello to Johnny.

At the same time Dad, at least as ill-at-ease as Johnny, it seemed, turned away to deal with his tears. Dad then approached John Michael, shook his hand, and said, "We-e-e-e-ll, hello there!" He immediately turned to Michelle and said, "And how are you, young lady?"

I felt ambushed and angry at the display, trembling angry. The moment Roger was free, I sidled over to him and said, "Did you see that?"

"Yep," he responded, uncharacteristically contained.

"What the hell was that all about? I travel from Minnesota and you come in from California to surprise him and we don't get half the emotion. We are his sons for God's sake. We're footing the bill!"

"Yep, that's our dad, Mike," Roger said. "The one who always says, 'I care.' Johnny idealizes him. He can deal with that. We know him as he really is. He can't deal with that."

Whammo! Nothing more needed to be said.

•　　•　　•

Johnny liked my pallbearer suggestion. "Okay, I'll check with Lillian," he said.

I had another idea. "John, there is something you could help with come to think of it. I am looking for a small brass band to play at the church or the cemetery. Do you think you could find one?"

"Sure. I can try."

"That would be great. When Dad was born, Grandpa had a brass band greet Grandma and Dad at the hospital. I thought it would be fun to have him go out as he came in."

"Sure." John was clearly happy to do it. "I'll see what I can do. I know some people. It can't be too difficult."

"Thanks, John. I appreciate it."

As Mom prepared dinner, Roger stood in the kitchen with her swapping stories. Joe lounged upstairs with a ball game.

"Well, what happened?" Mom asked.

I filled them in. We rehashed Dad's relationship with Johnny and the birthday party. Mom agreed with Roger's assessment. Both thought that pall bearer was the right role for Johnny and Jerry, his brother.

Because I valued wisdom and wished to grow in it, I had the long-standing habit of consulting about much that I did as a pastor and, though a little less, about my personal life as well. Wisdom dictated that I run the brass band plans before Mom and Rog. I hesitated. I like dramatic flair in ritual and preaching; Mom and Rog were less positively disposed. Always suspicious about my own plans when I am hesitant to share them, though, I decided to ask them.

"Hey, I have a question for the two of you. When Dad was born, Grandpa had Grandma and Dad met outside St. Joe's hospital with a brass band. I have asked Jeff Dames to get a little one for the funeral. What do you think?"

"Michael, no," Mom responded instantly. "That's corny."

"No, Mike," Rog immediately agreed.

I needed reasons. "I was thinking of just a little one, perhaps four or five instruments, perhaps at the cemetery or at church, playing *When the Saints Go Marching In* or something like that."

"No!" Mom said. "Mike, your grandfather was a goofball. He did all kinds of things like that, but that was in the thirties and forties. People don't do things like that today. People would think it was silly."

"No, Mike," Roger chimed in. "I don't think Lil or anybody else will get it either. You and I might. Gloria might. No one else will, though. It doesn't make any sense. It's hammy. Drop it."

"Are you sure? I thought it would be a nice touch."

"Yes," they responded in chorus.

I thought their reasons compelling. A band being passé didn't bother me; folks not getting it did. I knew they were right. "Well, if you will excuse me, I have to make a couple of phone calls."

I went to the office and called Dames Funeral Home. Jeff was not in, so I left a message with his secretary. John Michael picked up the phone. He accepted my reasoning and offered again to help in any way he could. I told him I appreciated his kindness and patience.

During dinner – pork tenderloin with all the trimmings – we talked about Michael, speculating on whether he would graduate from high school in June, or not. Roger seemed unsure. We discussed twelve-year-old Kristen, with her very focused care in maintaining two horses, five cats, and good grades. We reviewed the possibilities about Karen's finishing her occupational therapy degree and taking her board examinations in July. The meal was pleasant and easy. Joe retired to the TV while we did dishes.

As I put food away, Mom and Rog brought in the dirty dishes. So, I asked, "What do you think I should say about Dad in the preaching?" For thirty-six hours I had thought about the question but was still unsure. I knew talking about it would clarify my thoughts.

Roger, in a frisky mood, took my question as bait. "Well, Mike, you could say that he liked big cars."

"Yeah," Mom said taking the cue. "You could say that he re-e-e-eally liked sex, too."

"And it didn't matter whether it was alone or with others, either," Rog retorted.

We started laughing.

"Remember how he dealt cards with one hand?" Rog quipped. Mom immediately followed Roger's remark with an imitation.

"Or how he liked brown-and-white wing tips and used toothpicks to put white shoe polish in a-a-a-a-all those little holes!" Mom hunched her shoulders and bore down intently on imaginary holes in imaginary shoes.

I could hardly stop laughing. Mom and Rog were on a roll. Dad was quirky, to say the least, and we knew well all his quirks. Even a partial listing was hilarious, especially with illustrations. For the two of them nothing was too sacred for devastating comment and mimic. I enjoyed it, but I also needed serious help.

"Wait a minute, wait a minute, wait a minute, you two. I've got a problem here. I have to preach Dad's funeral. What should I say?" I had their attention. "I have been thinking about this. How about, since we are back at St. Joe's, the opener could be, 'Mickey Papesh has come home.'"

"Mike," Mom responded immediately. "He didn't care about those people at St. Joe's. He spent his whole life keeping his distance from them. He thought he was better than them."

"Really?" I instantly apprehended the forthright truth she spoke but felt caught off-guard and needed time with the thought. It pierced the bubble of what I might be able to say.

"Oh, yeah, Mike," Roger added. "He went to Florida to save face and didn't keep in touch with anybody except Mark and Sharon Dames, even though he lived in Joliet for fifty-four years."

"Okay," I said tentatively. "How about this? I could lead with his being welcomed by a brass band at birth, then talk about family and come to some meaning for his life that way."

"Yeah, you could do that," Mom said. "But his family life was turmoil. The Papeshes didn't have much of a family life because they were working at the tavern all the time."

•   •   •

Having lost his store in the Depression, Grandpa Papesh was working at a bowling alley in 1933 when he learned from a tavern-keeper friend that a building fell available just outside the Joliet city limits in an area called Crest Hill. The friend thought it would make a good tavern; it needed work, but it could go. So, Grandpa got together some money at the very high rate of eight percent from a silent partner, lawyer Henry Hammel, and began to work on the place. With two barrels of beer and three bottles of whiskey, Grandpa opened Longoda Tavern in late 1933 on old Route 66 just outside Joliet. The name was supposed to mean "watering hole" in a Native American language. Soon it became known simply as Mike Papesh's Tavern.

For thirty-six years, Grandpa Papesh worked the bar all day at the tavern, a half-chewed-half-smoked cigar always in his mouth. Warm, naturally gregarious, philosophical, and having a big heart that would buy anyone a drink or offer a fellow down on his luck $40 if he asked for $20, Grandpa gave the tavern its unique character and life. When silent film star Tom Mix once stopped by for a meal, for instance,

Grandpa had him bring in his horse, Tony. Dad remembered one time seeing an Indian motorcycle driven through his father's place. Once, a telephone pole was put through the windows on either side of the building by some of Grandpa's friends, blocking the hallway to the private rooms. A joke on the jokester.

The greatest attraction of Mike Papesh's Tavern was Grandpa spreading sawdust on the floor and doing "the shuffle" to music from the juke box. People loved it and sometimes got up to join in. Pictures show him in wide ties with his name on them, cowboy hats, Dutch shoes, a tuxedo, and always with one of his thirteen daily cigars in his smile. Grandpa was in his element at the tavern. In the 1960s, his teeth brown and configured to his cigar, Grandpa still cut an occasional tie or screwed a nickel into the floor, laughing as he watched people try to pick it up.

Mike Papesh's Tavern was popular in the 1930s and '40s. The chicken and steaks were excellent and cheap. Because the tavern was technically out in the country, people from both Joliet and Chicago drove to Papesh's on Route 66 after city closing hours, because Mike's was sure to be open. Even Joliet city fathers, including the sheriff, gathered there in the wee hours of the morning long after the place was supposed to have closed.

The tavern dominated Papesh family life. Often going to bed at three or four o'clock in the morning, long after Grandma, Grandpa got up and left home for the bank at ten o'clock each morning. He always packed his .38 revolver in the car with him – both to and from the bank, and particularly on Fridays when he carried the money that would cash customers' paychecks. He would arrive at the tavern to open by eleven o'clock, in time for the luncheon crowd. He stayed at the bar until the tavern closed.

Conversely, Grandma was a natural homebody who disliked work "out in the public," as she would say. But even she, starched and glistening in white from head to toe, would often help waitress. And she hated it. Dad, too, helped out at the tavern. From the time he was eight years old, Dad would go up to the tavern after school at four o'clock to wait on people in cars, and later in the tavern itself, serving food and beer. In cars and in the private rooms Dad saw far more than a youngster ought, he would say. He would finish work about nine-thirty, get to bed by ten o'clock, then be up for school in the morning.

Grandma hired a series of young girls to move into the house on Ruby Street to serve as nanny for Aunt Gloria when she was a baby, to care for Dad when he was at home, and to do some light housecleaning. Aunt Gloria followed a similar regime as Dad's when she turned twelve, old enough to wait on tables. Grandpa's father even helped at the tavern for a year, sweeping, mopping, and cleaning up. His Uncle Ignac did the same for eight years.

Work became the consuming focus of life for the Papeshes. Grandpa believed that the recipe for success was, "Work hard. Play dumb." Dad and Aunt Gloria learned this philosophy at his knee and followed it. The price was high.

Grandma complained often to Grandpa about his not spending time with the family. He tried to compensate by being generous with his money, buying the family fine clothes and treating them to occasional outings, like Riverview amusement park in Chicago. Family life grew increasingly fractured, however, as the years passed. Time together outside of work at the tavern gradually diminished to nearly nothing, which created great strain in a family where emotions were strongly felt, words could get blunt, and people were very easily hurt.

For instance, Dad once told me a story that, at fourteen, he went to the bar and asked his father if he could talk with him privately for a minute in room one.

From behind the bar Grandpa said, "What is it, Sonny?" He then came to the end of the bar, took out his wallet, opened it and reached for bills. "Do you need something, Sonny? Do you need some money?"

Dad, irate at this typical quick fix when it was the farthest thing from his mind, responded, "You can keep your goddamned money!" And he walked out.

Though he had no memory of what he wanted from his father that day, when Dad told the story at seventy years of age his hurt remained fresh. When I asked him what happened after he walked out, Dad responded, "Mom told me later that Dad was hurt."

Dad received no further response from Grandpa. Amid honest hard work, genuine laughter and good fun, mutual hurt piled big over the years.

Grandma grew especially resentful. On her fifty-seventh birthday in 1960, for instance, when we walked into the tavern, Grandma was crying. She and Grandpa had just had an argument and Grandpa had called her a vile name. As she wiped her tears, she hissed to the assembled family, "He's married to a goddammed saloon!"

Her remark captured the essence of Papesh family life.

•　　•　　•

Mom went on, "Then there was all the stress about money when your dad got into business. His mother felt so deprived when your grandfather lent your dad money."

•　　•　　•

Dad's entry into his own funeral business in 1952 shook the family's foundations. On one hand, his parents were proud of him. On the other, money tensions split the family.

In 1948, during his embalmer's apprenticeship, Dad bought a combination limousine and ambulance to earn side income. He and Mom had been living on her secretary's salary of $25 per week. Shortly after his apprenticeship ended, Dad quit his job and, for a time, tended bar at the tavern for $50 a week, doing ambulance work on the side. After two years of this pattern, Dad borrowed $2,000 from Mom's Great-Aunt Nell Jordan to have architectural plans drawn up for a funeral home. He never built it because the required zoning change fell through. In 1952 Dad bought a funeral business for $6,000 up front. Without consulting Grandpa, Dad borrowed the money from Henry Hammel. He paid $150 per month to rent the funeral home building – even as he kept up payments to Hammel for the loan.

Grandpa was furious. He yelled and tried to reason with Dad, but nothing would change his mind.

Then, while Dad was buying used furniture to get the funeral home ready for opening in August 1952, the Funeral Directors Association informed him that he could not open his doors unless he owned a hearse. Ambush! Having nowhere else to go, Dad went up to the tavern and asked Grandpa if he could help with the payments; he thought his parents had lots of money. Grandpa didn't like it, but it was too late for Dad to turn back and Grandpa wanted him to have a chance to succeed. Dad took out a loan to buy a 1948 Cadillac hearse for about $4,000 and Grandpa indulgently made the down payment and the monthly payment of $110.

The bite was too big for Grandma and Gloria.

Something of a "clothes horse" who liked nice things, Grandma had gotten used to Grandpa buying her most anything she wanted. The two of them indulged Gloria as well. They bought her stone martins at eighteen and a new engagement ring with larger diamonds after Uncle John proposed. They furnished the apartment upstairs on Ruby Street after Gloria and John married and let them live there rent free. The money for Dad's hearse meant that finances became tight. Grandma resented it. Gloria resented it. Family relationships grew tense.

As late as 1958, when Dad bought our first family home, a seven-room bungalow, the first time Grandma and Gloria stopped by, Gloria came into the house only briefly. Grandma remained out front in the car crying. Grandpa and Grandma had never owned their own home and both Grandma and Gloria suspected that Grandpa had helped Dad buy the house. Although he was still paying for the hearse, Grandpa had not given Dad a dime for the house. That night Gloria made excuses, but everyone knew that it was simply too painful for Grandma to come in.

• • •

"Mike, I don't think you ought to get into all that."

"Yeah, Mike, I think Mom's right," Rog added.

I felt stymied. "I am trying to find a way to say something in the preaching, but I don't know what to say. Dad was someone who had no great vice, but he also had no great virtue. I have thought about it for years, but I can't seem to figure out what readings to use, or what to say."

"Why do you have to say anything?" It was Mom again. "Don't preach."

"Really? Don't preach?" I was a competent preacher and well known for effective preaching at funerals. Not preaching Dad's funeral had failed to occur to me.

"Right. If you don't have anything to say, don't say anything," Mom quipped.

Mom's directness had Roger and I both thinking. He was wide-eyed, taking it all in, sitting at the kitchen table watching Mom at the counter. I could see that, though still processing Mom's words, Rog agreed.

"Wow! Not preach my own father's funeral." That was thinkable but hard to grasp. "Well, I suppose I could go that way. My peers sometimes do and sometimes don't. One guy prepared but had a back-up."

"People would understand," Mom added.

"Yeah, you're right." I was musing out loud. "They would think that grief kept me from preaching, not that I didn't have anything to say about my father."

71

"There's also a lot less risk, Mike," Roger chimed in, "with Lil and Gloria sitting there."

"Right," Mom jumped in. "Your experience of him is lots different from theirs. You know a side of him they wouldn't want to hear about. It's all about appearances, remember. What you would say about your dad probably wouldn't match their image of him, especially Lil's. And even if it did match in some places, like it might for Gloria, they wouldn't want you telling everybody about it. You risk getting yourself in lots of trouble. What can you say with them sitting there?"

"Yeah, you've got something there. I really couldn't say anything much that wouldn't risk getting them mad. It could get very touchy."

"Why take the risk?" Mom asked.

"Right." I could see Mom was calm, knowing that the direction of the conversation felt right. Roger seemed in solid agreement. "Well, I guess I have another call to make."

"George Klepec can do it. He didn't know your father," Mom said flatly.

"In fact, he did, though."

"But not like we do, Mike," Rog responded. "Let him do it."

"Okay. Wow! Not preach your own father's funeral because you have nothing to say. Wow!"

A little dazed, but knowing that the course was the correct one, I left the kitchen to call George Klepec at St. Joe's.

I phoned from upstairs. An answering machine took the call. "George, this is Michael Papesh. I have thought about it and, if you don't mind, could you concelebrate and preach my dad's funeral? I just can't do it. I hope that is okay with you. I am happy to preside, but I would appreciate your help in the preaching. Thanks."

I felt immediate relief. Preaching always caused anxiety and sweaty palms for me. Relinquishing it, for all the struggle it was to do so, took the anxiety out of Dad's funeral for me. I knew I had done the right thing.

I freshened up and went to the bathroom, then decided to call Gloria. She seemed all alone in the planning of this event, cut-off from Lil and from us. I could only guess what she knew. I told her the news about the re-arrangements.

"Thank God!" she responded. "Michael, I don't know what in the world Lillian was thinking. This is so much better, the way he would have wanted it. And I can't wait to hear what you are going to say."

"Gloria, I have decided not to preach. I just can't."

"Oh!" I could hear a tinge of disappointment. "That's okay. You have to think of yourself in all this, too."

"By the way, Gloria, can I ask you for some advice?"

"Sure." I heard her typical heartiness in her voice and took comfort in it.

I asked her opinion about the flowers. I spared her all my reasoning. "What do you think?"

"I think that's great." She meant it.

"Oh, okay, good."

"Well, Michael, it sounds like now my brother can rest in peace."

I went downstairs afterward and briefed the family. "Gloria was a little disappointed, I think, but accepted that I wasn't going to preach. I took that as a good sign."

"Oh, sure," Mom said. "They'll understand and be just fine with it."

"Oh, yeah, Mike. Everything will be fine," Roger agreed.

"It sure takes the pressure off," I said.

"That's great," Mom replied. "Your expectations are probably higher than theirs. Preaching at a time like this is lots to ask. You'll be much better off for this."

"I am starting to realize that Dad's funeral is not something I do, but it is *for me*."

"That's right, Mike. That's the way it ought to be."

"Well," Joe said, entering the kitchen. "Is it time to tour the new building yet?"

I had forgotten. I showed the three of them around thoroughly. After we got back to the rectory, we talked a little about various things, then went to bed.

As I lay in bed, I could hardly believe that I not only wasn't preaching my father's funeral, but I couldn't. Surely, though, there must be something I could say. Perhaps a eulogy…

CHAPTER V
More Reality: Struggling to Let Be

I got up Saturday morning and performed my usual ritual of cleaning up, walking, and feeding the dogs, setting the table for breakfast, and praying. We would, I expected, eat around eight o'clock. That was Mom and Joe's usual schedule at their Colorado ranch. Without morning Mass, I found the schedule easy to keep. Roger would fit in whenever he arose. He rarely ate breakfast anyway. Just before eight o'clock the phone rang.

"Hello, Mike? This is George Klepec."

"Hi, George. Did you get my message?"

"Yes. I am happy to preach your dad's funeral. I knew him for many years. He was very kind. Years ago, I spent time at your grandfather's place, too. We had lots of fun."

"Neat, George. Thanks. I appreciate it very much."

"Oh, you're welcome. Now, he died in Florida?" We were down to business. It was a natural move for a priest and infinitely easier between two priests since we both knew exactly what was happening and why.

"Yes, but Lil is in Illinois."

"Lil is his second wife, right? They are together?"

"Oh, yes. They lived in Florida. She was making a brief visit here to see her mother. Dad was healthy so she thought everything would be okay. She was a Kobe. Her mother is Ann Kobe. Lil was married to

75

Bill Bozich for about twenty years or so." Since he was trying to make connections I wanted to be as helpful as possible.

"How is your mother?" I was a little surprised by the question, but this was the first of many times I would be asked it in the next days.

"Oh, she is just fine, George. In fact, she is here. We have just built a $6 million parish center attached to the back of the school and we are dedicating it this weekend. The Archbishop will be here to dedicate it. She and her husband came up for the celebration."

"I remember her well. Give her my regards."

"I will, George."

"You remember your grandparents with fondness?" I thought the question oddly worded even if asked in a matter-of-fact way, suggesting assent. I wondered if it was a vague allusion to the history all the Slovenians knew but no one talked about.

"Oh, yes. Grandpa died in 1971, Grandma in 1985. She was a Vesel. She also died of Alzheimer's. I remember them very fondly."

"Your dad died of Alzheimer's, huh?"

"Yeah, George. He'd had it since he was sixty-nine. It progressed slowly at first but steadily. This past year-and-a-half he spent mumbling to himself in a wheelchair in a nursing home. He was a proud peacock of a man. It was very hard for him."

"He had been in Florida how long?"

"Just short of twenty-three years. They moved there in late summer of 1978."

"Okay, well that's all," he said, somewhat absent-mindedly.

I imagined him at his desk bent over a small sheet of paper, writing. He was collecting information for the preaching and doing it in the classic Slovenian way. Slovenes started slightly off-center, spun round and round about relationships until everything was gleaned, then the bull's eye falls into place without having to speak to it directly, which in this case was probably something like: "How does everyone get on?" I heard hours and hours of Dad and Grandma talking in circles like this. It drove Mom crazy. Roger would get bored and leave. I usually felt dazed by it but would sit and listen. Traveling to Slovenia in 1991, I was stunned to find that when I asked questions, I received the same kind of spinning, circular answers every time.

"We meet on Tuesday at a quarter after nine, right?" He went on.

"Yes, George, if that's okay with you. Roger and I will be there."

"That works for me. It's after my morning Mass. By the way, it costs extra to have *Cecenye Maria* sung in Slovenian. Our organist can't sing in Slovenian so we have to hire someone who can."

"That's fine, George. Just let Dames' know." I also assumed that Lil would pay that expense since it was her request.

"Okay, I'll do that. Well, see you Tuesday, Mike."

"Great, George. Thanks. See you then."

• • •

I had never presided at Mass at St. Joe's. At the time of my ordination in Minnesota, Mom lived in Colorado, Dad in Florida, and Roger in California. Grandma Papesh was ill with Alzheimer's. No close-in family members were available to plan the ceremonies or work things out with the community there. I felt self-conscious about pushing it and thought it a burden to try. To my surprise, the largest gift I received from outside the family came from the former pastor there, Msgr. Butala. He had been Grandpa's grade school classmate, took his assignment in the parish when Dad was in second grade and, though he retired in 1974, had remained at St. Joe's until he died at ninety-eight years old. The gift was $300. St. Joe's and the Slovenian community always held some nostalgia for me as a pastor. I affixed the parish keys onto a St. Joseph key ring.

I went down for breakfast to find Joe at the table with Mom. I greeted them and, after cutting myself some bread and pouring a diet cola, I went to the table and filled them in on the conversation with George.

"It sounds like the right thing, Mike," Joe observed.

"Aren't you relieved?" Mom asked. "Now you can just relax."

"Yes, I am. But I can't believe it."

We talked about the day ahead, especially lunch at White Castle – a rare treat for them – and roast beef for supper with the Archbishop after Mass. Roger came in during the discussion and sat at the end of the table. He had a cup of coffee and waved off anything else. His presence took the conversation into all kinds of things, typical family talk for us. Unpredictable fun.

After breakfast Joe left for upstairs. The three of us stayed behind to clear and do dishes.

"Hey, I have been thinking of something else," I began.

"Now what?" Mom said, her right hand on her hip with a worldly wise, expectant smile.

"Since I am not preaching, I thought about doing a eulogy at the end."

"What do you mean by *eulogy*?" Roger asked.

"At the end I would ask everyone to sit down, then I could thank them for coming and talk about Dad's life."

"You could do that," Mom said. "But are you sure you want to?"

"What do you mean?" I felt defensive. Here we go again, I thought.

"What stories would you tell?" She sensed what was in me.

"Well, I could talk about Dad's birth and the band at the hospital, and then tell the stories about his life."

"Why would you want to do that?" Mom asked.

Roger looked very much on alert. "Well, I think I should say something," I responded.

"Mike, look," she began in earnest. "They all know those stories. The people who will be there not only know the stories, they still live them every day of their lives. Mike, you are the stranger. Why should you come in and tell them stories they live with every day?"

The stories Mom meant, I knew, were three. Everyone there who knew the family would hear whatever I said through the filter of these stories. Shame filled them for us as a family, and Dad had worked all his life to get beyond them.

•   •   •

Grandpa Papesh quit fourth grade at ten years of age in 1908 to work at the American Steel and Wire Company with his father and his Uncle Ignac. The family needed his help for their support. In his first job he counted bolts. By the time of Great War draft registration, Grandpa registered as a grocer. He worked at a store on Broadway St., across the street from Vesel's. By January 1924, he had saved enough to make a down payment to buy, for $10,000, a small grocery store just three blocks from home. He called the place "Papesh Cash Grocery." He lived above the store.

At the store, during its first year, Grandpa fell in love with Anna Vesel, one of his clerks. After a whirlwind romance, they married August 26, 1924. On their wedding day, *The Spectator* captured Grandpa's natural ebullience. Under the heading, "Advertises Wedding and Gets Crowd," followed by, "West Side Grocer Marries While Hundreds Crowd Church Auditorium," the article read:

> 'Papesh takes a partner' and 'Roses for everybody' proved the truth of the old saw, 'It pays to advertise' this morning when the biggest crowd ever gathered in the church overflowed the spacious auditorium of St. Joseph's Catholic Church, North Chicago Street.
>
> The occasion was the wedding of M. Papesh, Hickory Street grocer, and his clerk, Miss Anne Vesel, 1149 North Broadway. It was the first advertised wedding in Joliet, and it brought returns by the hundreds.

MICHAEL LEO PAPESH

For more than a week 'Mike' Papesh has been advertising that 'Papesh takes a partner,' and several other expressions relating to the forthcoming event. Yesterday the enterprising young merchant came out with the announcement that 'There'll be roses for everybody at my wedding at St. Joseph's church tomorrow morning at eight o'clock.'

If 'everybody' wasn't there it wasn't the fault of Mike who called greetings to hundreds of friends and hundreds of strangers as the happy couple worked a way thru the throngs who were unable to gain admittance to the ceremony. According to the Rev. John Plevnik, pastor of St. Joseph's church, it was the largest crowd the church had seen in thirty years.

At the home of the bride, 1149 North Broadway, where a wedding breakfast was being served to half a hundred guests, 'Mike' beamed all over as he surveyed the crowd outside the house. And then he sighed as he shook his head.

'If I only had the room to feed 'em I could have ten thousand up here as well as not,' he mourned as he untied another bale of roses.

A cortege of automobiles moved away from the home as the bridal pair left for a motor trip. On the rear end of each machine were such classic inscriptions as 'Papesh has done it,' 'Papesh and company, wedded bliss and groceries.'

In the wedding pictures, the twenty-six-year-old groom has an open and smiling face, appearing confident and self-possessed. He leans toward both his bride and the camera. The bride, her ankles crossed and feet up on her left high heel, looks elated and completely at ease. Bouquets of roses sit at their feet. Uncle Edward Vesel and Aunt Ann Papesh stood up for them. Everyone beams from ear to ear.

The Papeshes lived above the store when Dad was born. Grandma cared for the baby upstairs while Grandpa built his business downstairs. In 1926, he expanded the building to nine apartments up and six thousand square feet of store at the street. He faced the building with brick and had his name and the year of the renovation cast in cement on the parapet. Though the building burned to the ground February 2, 1970, and remained a vacant lot afterwards, in 1977 the *Joliet Herald-News* wrote of the renovated store's grand opening fifty years before:

> Lasting twelve hours, one of the largest festivals in the history of Joliet was held January 22 to celebrate completion of the new $35,000 addition to the Michael Papesh grocery, 1101-03 Hickory St., with more than eight thousand persons taking part in the festivities. During the night, twelve thousand bottles of pop, fourteen thousand sandwiches and fifteen thousand cups of coffee were served by a corps of thirty-five young women, and two six-piece orchestras were kept busy providing music for the dancers.

The picture of the event shows mostly men jammed in the furniture-less new addition of the store.

By the time Dad was able to walk, Grandpa had forty-three employees and five red delivery trucks. He drove a 1924 Willys-Knight DeLuxe. He was a fun-loving clown of a man with a nose for publicity. For instance, at the time of Dad's birth, Grandpa displayed his new buggy in the store window for three months prior. Grandpa also put three-year-old Mickey's picture in the newspaper wearing a three-piece tweed suit, his first long pants. In a brief notice underneath the dapper Mickey, Dad is quoted as saying that he is certain he wants to be a grocer when he grows up, just like his dad.

Grandpa lost everything between April 28, 1931, when the Joliet National Bank foreclosed on the store, and on October 13, 1931, when it foreclosed on the last of his land. He had over-stretched himself while trying to build the business. He had also continued delivering groceries even when his customers, Slovenian people from Joliet's north side, had no money to pay the bills. In the mid-1940s, the boxes of the store's accounts, found in the old barn next to the smoke house in the back yard of Ruby Street, were thrown out. Grandma told Dad, away in the South Pacific at the time, that she tallied the old bills before the tossing and people owed Grandpa over $90,000. "And you wouldn't believe the names on the lists!" she often reported over the years.

Grandpa lost his mother in June 1931. Aunt Gloria Ann was born September 20, 1931. Both events occurred in between the foreclosures. That same year Grandpa declared bankruptcy, a public humiliation that left a permanent blot on his reputation. From then until his death, Dad and Gloria's names were on all deeds. Grandpa officially owned nothing. His world collapsed all at once and Gloria was born in the ashes.

As I listened to Mom, I knew that the Slovenian community would remember Grandpa's bankruptcy and talk about it in whispers. Why he went bankrupt, though, remained unspeakable among them.

When Dad was seventy-one, he finally admitted that, during this same period, Grandpa owned part of a still and black market liquor business. It was Prohibition. Grandpa and his partner had a shack out in the country on the northwest side of town, near the Guardian Angels

Home – an orphanage – where they kept the still. Even when he finally spoke of the operation after years of making dismissive comments, Dad made light of it. He defensively noted that his Petan cousins had a still in their basement, as did many others during Prohibition. It failed to register for Dad that Grandpa's still may have been a different kind of operation than a home still. I learned from cousins that as early as 1924, Grandpa's brother, Uncle Anton, called "Doc," used to make runs during the night delivering liquor to speakeasies in town. Doc always carried a gun.

In 1932, Grandpa got wind around the Joliet speakeasies that his partner in the still business was cheating him. He decided to visit Charlie at the still one night, his .38 revolver in hand, to have a talk. Whether it was a set-up or not we will never know, but the police raided the still that night. Charlie fled in his car. Grandpa took off on foot through the woods. Dad remembered Grandpa coming home with mud up to his knees, torn and tousled. He was furious, waving the .38 and saying, "If I ever catch that son-of-a-bitch I am going to kill him!"

The next day Grandpa was arrested. He served three months in detention. Dad remembered his father sitting on the front steps of the place when Uncle Ed Vesel drove Grandma and him up to Geneva to visit Grandpa there.

Whatever vague sense of guilt and sympathy the Slovenian community may have felt because of Grandpa's bankruptcy, they surely felt less of it when he got caught bootlegging. In the family, Grandpa's serving time besmirched his reputation so terribly that no one talked about it. The original tip-off about the jail time seeped into my immediate family in the 1950s through Mom's mother, not the Slovenian family. When Dad finally addressed it after I gently probed him, I felt surprised that Dad talked about it, even defensively. Gloria never uttered a word. Did she know?

These two events in Grandpa's life, for all their seriousness, could still be explained away and sympathetically understood by the Slovenian community. Not the third event, which sealed an indelible stain on Grandpa's reputation and remained a struggle for Dad all his life.

Grandpa's father, also Michael Martin Papesh, was killed by a car on Broadway Street, old Route 66 going through Joliet. The December 19, 1936, *Joliet Herald-News*, under the headline "Two Pedestrians Killed by Autos," reads in part:

> Papesh was struck by an auto driven by George Gray, 105 West Park Avenue. He told Sheriff's officers that Papesh loomed in front of him and was struck before he could stop his car.
>
> Both were heading south on North Broadway. The body was found on the shoulder of the road, and Gray's car stopped within several feet of the accident. He told officers he had been moving slowly just before the mishap.
>
> Papesh was rushed to St. Joseph's hospital by William M. Hart, 107 Sherwood Place, who passed the scene and was flagged by Mr. Gray. Papesh was dead upon arrival.
>
> His family stated that he was returning home after visiting the tavern of his son, Mike Papesh Jr., 2306 North Broadway.

The accident happened about 5:30 P.M. on December 18. Great-Grandpa Papesh died of multiple skull fractures. The coroner declared the accident unavoidable.

According to Grandma, his father's body was "hardly cold" when Grandpa flew down to his lawyer, who was also Grandpa's silent partner in the tavern, and had a will drawn up. The will, one page long, left everything to Grandpa, the oldest son and third of five living children, and to Dad and Gloria. Grandpa was also named executor. An unsteady 'X' marked Great-grandpa's signature. The will, dated January 2, 1935, was witnessed by John Malnar, Grandpa's best friend, and Clark Hously, the tavern cook.

After their father's funeral, Grandpa's brother and sisters wanted to know what their part of the inheritance would be. Dad remembered a loud argument at the Ruby St. Papesh homestead on a Sunday morning. Grandpa threw his sisters and brother out, all of them still yelling at each other. This inheritance squabble developed into a full-blown family feud.

January 9, 1937, with Grandpa's sister Theresa Rose already dead and his oldest sister, Aunt Mary, staying out of it – her step-father had given her the gift of a vacant Joliet lot in 1935 – Grandpa's sisters Antonia and Ann and his brother Tony petitioned the court to have the estate administered immediately because their father had left no will. The petition for administration of the will, which Grandpa had in hand, was filed three days later, January 12. Then the fight began.

In court documents, Grandpa valued the estate at $270. His brother and sisters valued it at $2,000. Probation notices were published twice in 1937 and twice the will was contested in hearings. In January 1938, Grandpa petitioned the court for $667.49 for his expenses. Legalities then sat silent for nineteen years until a third set of probation notices was published in the fall of 1957. The will was settled May 2, 1960. After living in the house with his family for over twenty-five years, Grandpa received the deed for the house, several vacant lots in the city that Great-Grandma had used for gardens, and his $667.49 for expenses. Grandpa sold the house that same year for $5,000. Most of the lots were sold over the next nine years because

Grandpa was strapped for cash that he needed to keep the tavern running and pay off his silent partner.

The results of the family feud were far-reaching. Tonka, Ann, Tony, and their spouses and children never again spoke to Grandpa.

Sometime soon after the house was sold, I remember going with Grandpa to John Malnar's barber shop on Broadway. Little did I know then that I was with two parties to the events. During my haircut, with a head nod toward the picture window, Grandpa asked John, "Hey, do you ever see that one, across the street?"

"Tonka? Yes, occasionally," John responded.

Grandpa said wistfully, "Life's too short. She ought to let go of the past."

As the family story has it, Antonia remained especially bitter. When she died in 1966, Tonka was buried from Racki Funeral Home, right across Ruby St. from the family homestead. Dad, then at Dames Funeral Home as partner and manager, asked Steve Racki to open the funeral home during off-hours so Grandma, Mom, and Dad could pay their respects and sign the register. I can only imagine Tonka's family's reaction right before the wake to the surprise signatures in the register. Grandpa remained at the tavern.

Through the years, Grandpa continued to communicate with Aunt Mary. He loaned her some money and she went to the tavern each month to make the $50 repayment. She also discussed with him family cemetery plots and released her claim. These occasions were strictly business, however. Aunt Mary came to Grandpa's funeral in 1971, but when she died four years later, she was buried from Tezak Funeral Home, not Fred C. Dames. Grandpa was mentioned in Aunt Mary's obituary, as he was in Tonka's, Ann's, and Tony's, but little more remained among them than bitterness.

Grandpa's brothers and sisters let it be known far and wide in the Slovenian community that they had been cheated out of their inheritance. Grandpa's reputation in the Slovenian community hit bottom and never lifted. Through all the years Grandpa owned it, the Slovenian people never much went to Mike Papesh's Tavern, nor did Grandpa's family. His business came from the railroad, the steel mill, the rubber plant and, after legal closing hours, from the Joliet city fathers.

In response to the cold shoulder from the Slovenians, Grandpa withdrew from them. Though he sent an envelope to church each week with Grandma, who assisted at Mass faithfully and served on many church committees, Grandpa never attended church or parish functions. Grandpa's absence only deepened the damage in an ethnic, inbred Catholic parish community known in Slovenian circles as *Slovenski Rim*, the Slovenian Rome, whose pastor was Grandpa's grade school classmate.

●　　●　　●

My family experience of the Slovenian community told me that they loved to tell stories about their own. They remembered. So, Mom's perspective sounded reasonable. I knew Dad carried Grandpa's reputation as a burden because Dad's funeral business was based in the Slovenian community. After he began the business, in fact, he once said to Mom, "Mary Jean, my dad's reputation in the Slovenian community is terrible."

I still felt I needed to say something. So, a little defensively, I said to Mom, "I suppose you're right. I'll think about it."

"Do what you want, but they know the stories better than you do. It's not worth what it will probably cost you in the end."

CHAPTER VI
A Dedication and a Birthday

I spent the rest of Saturday morning fussing over the weekend dedication celebration, checking out the details in the church and in the commons, gymnasium, and kitchen of the new Pentecost Hall. By late morning, everything seemed to be in order but for flowers. At eleven-thirty, Mom, Joe, Rog, and I enjoyed lunch at White Castle then went back to the rectory to rest.

Nervous about the upcoming events, I ducked over to check messages at the office. There was one. The Archbishop's secretary called to let me know that the Archbishop, stranded in the Detroit airport, couldn't make it for four o'clock Mass. Like Dad, persnickety about details day-to-day but balanced and creative in a crisis, I spent the next two hours modifying an old Pentecost homily so I could preach at four o'clock. After clean up, confessions, and some nervous preparation in the sacristy, the Pentecost Eucharist felt exultantly festive and the homily fit the occasion. Mom, Joe, and Rog, attentive in the front pew, later affirmed my impression.

After Mass I went back to the office to check phone messages. There was one. "Father Michael, this is Archbishop Flynn. I was stranded at the airport, but I am now home. I just wanted to let you know that I will be on hand for your dedication tomorrow at... let's see... ten-thirty. I will see you then."

I felt a surge of anxiety. The dedication was scheduled for ten o'clock. My memory flashed that I had saved the Archbishop's home phone number some years ago when he published it. I had never used it but thought it might come in handy someday. Now was the day. I dared to dial the number.

"Hello, this is Archbishop Flynn."

I couldn't believe it. I had never called an Archbishop at home, and he picked up the receiver on the first ring! "Archbishop, this is Father Michael Papesh."

"Oh, hello, Father Michael. I am so sorry I could not make it this afternoon. I was stuck in the Detroit airport. Did you get my message?"

"Yes, I did, Archbishop. Thank you. I am calling to let you know that the Mass tomorrow morning is at ten, not ten-thirty."

"Oh! I am so glad you called." He paused for a moment. "Yes, it says right here ten o'clock." I had sent him about twenty-one pages worth of instructions containing the whole ritual order and texts. "Now where did I get ten-thirty?"

"The time represents a change from our normal schedule. Perhaps you looked it up in the Archdiocesan directory." It was a priest's job to take care of his bishop. "But when I heard you say ten-thirty in the message, I certainly wanted to call to let you know the correct time. It would be a shame if you were late."

"Oh, yes, Father Michael. I couldn't agree more. Thank you for calling." A wonderful man, though not much of an administrator, nor one who took much stock in making sure things were in the right order, the Archbishop cared deeply about how I felt and the contributions of the janitor to the celebration. One of the priests offered the droll summary of all the priests' sentiments when he remarked, "Try as hard as I can, I cannot not like him." He radiated charity.

"You're welcome, Archbishop."

"I'll see you tomorrow at ten o'clock."

My Papesh fussbudget was hooked again. "Perhaps nine-thirty, Archbishop? You can park on Albert Street in front of the new parish center. A space will be marked for you there." I had to be sure.

"Oh, very good. I will see you tomorrow at nine-thirty."

Was the dedication cursed? I wondered.

I walked back across the street for supper. Mom, Joe, Roger, and I feasted on Mom's roast beef dinner. Our talk was light and scattered and remained so in the living room for the rest of the evening.

As we chatted on the living room floor, Roger and I cleaned seven brass and silver medallions depicting the gifts of the Holy Spirit that the notoriously procrastinating artist delivered that morning. Right at the border of his powers in his early seventies, he had left glue and residue on the silver cutouts of the Spirit's gift symbols and on the brass medallions themselves. Roger and I wiped the silver edges down with alcohol. When we finished, Rog, Mom, Joe, and I each took a medallion or two and went over to the commons to hang them. As the family walked back to the rectory, I placed and watered flowers in the gym.

The next morning, we all ate breakfast together. Nervous about the dedication, I excused myself at eight-thirty to patrol the spaces for a final details review. I then conducted the ushers' practice for the dedication. The ushers were our very best. Everything was set.

The Archbishop pulled in at nine-thirty. Still sitting in his car, he said, "Now, Father Michael, you told me to bring a gold crosier, is that right?" He was pulling in slowly as if ready to pull out and retrieve another if I asked for a silver one.

"Yes, Archbishop, a gold crosier." I had specified that detail in the letter to him, wanting his shepherd's staff to match the vestments.

"Oh, very good. I brought Archbishop Binz's." That Archbishop was his predecessor three times removed, remembered as "Tilly Binz" for his stiff, lacey propriety. Crosiers were something bishops passed on, I gathered.

I took up the Archbishop's suitcase and crosier case, and we walked into the parish center conference room where he was to vest. His red vestment with a canary yellow yoke and brass-gold trim was laid out for him.

"Oh, Father Michael, this is a lovely vestment! Now tell me," he reached into his suitcase and produced three folded miters in clear plastic cases, placing each of them on the vestment. "Which one of these do you think would go best?" One hat was white, one red, one white with gold brocade. I had suggested a white one in the letter.

"Archbishop, I think the red one goes very well." It was close in color and I knew he would prefer that one to the others. He was more careful about his appearance than running the Archdiocese. Still, truer to form than I had imagined, he was stunningly thoughtful and kindly gracious to bring three miters and offer me a choice.

"Very fine. That's the one I'll wear."

I helped him vest. As I placed the chasuble on him, he said, "Tell me, Father. Were these vestments here when you came, or did you have to buy them?" He was evidently impressed by the richness of the chasuble.

"I had to buy them, Archbishop. What was here was inferior and they were used only for Sunday Mass. Weekdays I was expected to wear only a stole over an alb. I just couldn't do that. I use those vestments for weekdays and bought new for Sundays."

"It was like that when I went to St. Ambrose." He had been pastor for a brief three years in New York state before becoming a bishop in Louisiana. He loved to talk about those years, and I imagined him a smash hit as a pastor. He added, "The iconoclasts had thrown them out." An ordinarily witty and joyful Irishman, the Archbishop had an ideologically conservative undercurrent that unbecomingly surfaced on occasion. I said nothing. As he went out to greet the deacons and servers, I vested, then walked across the street to the church.

Promptly at ten o'clock, I gave housekeeping instructions to the assembly of some six-hundred-fifty. Given the movement within the ritual, they needed to know what was coming if the ceremony was to move smoothly. Introductions of special guests followed: the architect and his staff, the construction firm and their staff, the council members, parish pastoral staff and school faculty.

Then, without warning them, I introduced Joe, Mom, and Rog. I could tell that the three of them felt thrilled. Though they heard plenty of stories from me over the years, the family rarely shared in my being a priest. I also knew the parishioners would be pleased to have them there, and even more pleased, some of them, to corner Mom, Joe, and Rog later. The folks applauded them heartily.

The ceremony was lavish and spiritually transporting. Given the tumult in the parish that had come with building the addition and taking on a huge debt, this liturgy bore a heavy burden and did it well. The music, with choir, cantors, organ, and brass, was lush and rich, worthy of a cathedral. The deacons, servers and ushers executed their roles precisely. The Archbishop preached eloquently on the themes I had suggested: communion, stewardship, and mission. He thanked the people for doing something beautiful for Jesus.

The trickiest part of the ceremony worked; we remained prayerful, sustained our singing, and did not break ritual through two extended processions, one from the church to the parish center under the Litany of the Saints, then one from the commons into the gym under organ and brass. The liturgy was one of those rare celebrations when worship does exactly what it is supposed to do: proclaim God's great gifts, extol the peoples' work, and effect God's grace and healing power in the assembly. The liturgy was so high church anyone could have gotten a nosebleed. The event would stand out, I knew, as a once-in-a-generation experience for the parish and a once-in-a-lifetime experience for me. I felt deeply moved, proud of the phalanx of parish staff and people who brought everything together so superbly.

One gaffe popped. At the end, when the Archbishop thanked everyone, including the janitors, for their contribution, he turned to

Mom, Joe and Roger and said, "And, Mrs. Papesh, thank you for coming all this way with your two sons for this celebration, even after the death of your husband. It is wonderful that you could be here with us."

Mom offered a wince of endurance. Joe and Roger were wide-eyed. I had not introduced them to the Archbishop ahead of time: I made no mention of them in fact. The parishioners knew the family history because of my years of preaching, so they were conscious of the mistake. The Archbishop evidently had heard they were in attendance and had heard mention of Dad's death in the Prayers of the Faithful, but he missed some nuances.

When the Archbishop was divesting later, I clarified the facts for him since he would be meeting the family shortly. I also suggested that he might be able to use the story of what happened as an amusing anecdote about the current state of the American family and our inability to predict anything in our time. He took the clarification and suggestion with a smile.

Stripped down to his French-cuffed, collarless shirt, he said, "Now, Father, I can only stay for twenty minutes but I brought my cassock and sash. If you would help me on with it, I will get out there and greet the people."

Because of the stress in the community during recent months, including not only the new building and debt, but also our moving toward full cost parochial elementary school tuition, I had asked the Archbishop by letter if he might appear at the reception in his regalia rather than in a suit. I thought he would cut a fine figure in black and purple and the people would be more fully impressed by the power of his presence. He was again accommodating my request in a near heroic way. He obviously took very seriously the healing work that he might be able to do on this day and brought all the equipment to make it happen. He put on his black cassock and, as I knelt on the floor buttoning him up from the bottom, he buttoned from the top. I was delighted to help.

He wore a fuchsia beanie, sash, buttons and trim with a black cassock and silver pectoral cross. He looked stunning. The folks loved it.

After greeting most everyone for twenty-five minutes, including Mom, Joe and Roger, the Archbishop swung around into the main offices to get ready for his next engagement. As he took off his regalia and donned his black suit, I raised my concern about the parish's unsettledness. "Archbishop, I want to let you know that you will soon be getting some letters about Holy Spirit. A parishioner, supported by the person who saw you in your office, is beginning a letter writing campaign to protest my approving change orders and permitting cost overruns."

On one level, I knew I had nothing to fear from the Archbishop. My pastorate was secure. Nonetheless, I felt embarrassed by the letter writing and insecure about my budget-breaking construction change orders and how they had resulted in the cost overrun. I also felt self-conscious about the kernel of truth regarding my direct and sometimes intimidating administrative style that lurked underneath the heated language and exaggerated claims in the letters I had already seen.

"Oh, Father Michael, I am glad you brought that up. I wanted to say something to you about that. I wrote him about joining the Serra Club and he wrote back about his disillusionment with the Catholic Church. I offered to meet with him to discuss that. When he came, he filled me with all kind of things that I hadn't expected…"

I cut him short. "Archbishop, you needn't go into details. I trust you completely with whatever happened in all that. I just wanted to let you know that there is some tumult here and you will be hearing about it." I really did trust completely his good intentions and pastoral instincts.

"Well, don't let that bother you one bit. I have been here. The spirit here is just wonderful. They love it. You have nothing to worry about, Michael. There are always naysayers in situations like this. Don't think a thing about it."

The parish had certainly heard in the Archbishop's preaching his strident support and deep gratitude for their generosity. I personally appreciated his assurances and felt touched and humbled by his unequivocal support despite my mistakes. The parish had what it needed from him; I had what I needed. He had done wonderfully apt ministry among us and for us. "Thank you, Archbishop. I am deeply grateful."

I accompanied the Archbishop to his car, then went back to the reception in the commons. For the next two hours I heard how wonderful the ceremony was, how marvelous the new building was, how great the reception was, and what a delight Mom was. I was so engaged by people that I had no time to eat.

Mom, Joe, and Rog escaped early, about one-thirty or so, to go over to the house and have some soup. I joined them about a quarter after three when I finished. They were as delighted and impressed by the ceremony as anyone else.

"Mike, even though we were in a gym, it felt just like church. And the procession from the church all the way across the street felt spiritual," Roger said. The event was no McDonald's hamburger if it touched Roger spiritually.

"The Archbishop is a wonderful man," Mom said. "I could listen to him all day."

"What about his gaffe? Some mistake, huh?" I couldn't resist hearing what they had to say about it.

"It's no big deal," Mom said.

"Oh, you just let that run off your back," Joe said matter-of-factly.

"And he made you my brother!"

"Yes," Joe responded with a smile and affected sweetness. "That's because I look so young."

We verbally took everything about the celebration apart and put it back together again for a while until it was about time to go for supper. I excused myself to shower and change.

LEADING MICKEY HOME

As I dressed, I thought about how much Dad would have liked the ceremony. He would have appreciated the work it took to get everything in its place, been touched by the experience itself, and felt proud for my part in orchestrating it. I also felt relieved the ceremony was over. Now I could begin to really focus on Dad's funeral. Now, perhaps, sadness would come.

After the shower, I snuck Mom's birthday gift into the car. We left for the restaurant at a quarter after five, arriving at five-thirty. The restaurant choice acquiesced to Joe. His pickiness about food, coupled with his assumption that a restaurant that veered from his personal culinary preferences was objectively a trough, left us with Southern Italian food as the safest choice. Mom was more democratic in her preferences, so were Roger and me. The success of her birthday dinner, however, rested on Joe's being content.

He was not. Taken far to the rear of the restaurant, to an area with long tables likely set for larger groups who had been there earlier, Joe grew wary about noise and whiny about our placement. Roger and I laid back as Mom tried to calm him. In the hope of helping, I risked the placid observation that the people already seated were adults, we had arrived early and most of the tables were vacant. It may have helped. He calmed.

Seated near a doorway with the door propped open also grew contentious. In Minnesota spring, when turning on the air-conditioning or leaving it off is guesswork, the management had left it off. The door propped open was necessary for the comfort of everyone in the room. Hating drafts, Joe believed in principle that an open door meant a draft, no matter the facts. Some sparring ensued between Joe and the waitress. Ultimately a compromise was reached; the door was closed but left ajar.

Then came the discussion about what to eat. Joe had been adamant on Thursday that he would pay on Sunday. I knew he would remain unbudgeable on the point. Because he was paying, however, I also knew that he aimed to make sure we ordered as inexpensively as possible. Joe begrudgingly settled ultimately on two entrees for the four of us and condescended to Roger and I having a glass of Chianti.

Then, when the waitress came to take the order, Joe asked if there were tomatoes on the salad. Fanatically attached to his daily fix, he had to have tomatoes. After an extended discussion in which the waitress took lightly this most resolute of requests, Joe got his tomatoes. We nearly had to open the door again to cool after the exchange. Mom, who was to my mind too accepting of Joe's churlish behavior at a restaurant table simply because she was so accustomed to it, finally ended it. She was the only one who had the power. "Happy Birthday to you, too!" She meaningfully snapped at Joe.

The meal, now on course, was delightful. The food was excellent, and we had fun conversation. At dessert, Roger and I gave cards to Mom and to Joe, Mom for her birthday, Joe for Father's Day, one from Roger and me, and one from the dogs, so Joe got two. I went to the car, then Rog and I presented her with three Baccarat butterflies, each a different color. Mom was thrilled.

"Not too shabby," Joe remarked.

In the setting sun, we drove home to sit around the rectory living room awhile, then prepare to leave for Illinois in the morning. I went to sleep exhilarated by the dedication, happy that Mom liked her gift and singing to myself the Requiem.

CHAPTER VII
Down Wisconsin with Roger

Early Monday morning we rose, ate breakfast, and then departed down Interstate 35E and Interstate 94 for Joliet, Illinois. Joe and I drove. Roger traveled with me, Mom with Joe. I suggested we meet at the Sun Prairie exit near Madison for lunch at the A&W there, and everyone agreed. I felt relieved to be driving out of town, free now to focus on Dad's funeral. I was especially happy to have Roger alone. I wanted the extended time with him.

"Did it ever occur to you in the last twenty-five years, Rog, that we would be traveling with Mom and Joe to Dad's funeral?"

"Nope. Never."

"Did it ever occur to you that Joe would be paying for part of Dad's casket?"

"No, Mike, it didn't."

And we were off on a four-hour talk about Dad and our upbringing.

• • •

In late 1949, Mom decided it was time to have a family. She had always wanted to have children, stay home with them, and be taken care of by her spouse. Her sense of the ideal size for a family was four children.

Dad resisted having children. Three years into their marriage, he felt too much in flux to have a child, too preoccupied. Besides, he really didn't like children. He needed order and a sense of control over his environment. He grew impatient and testy when things were out of order. Children brought disorder.

In 1948, two years married, Dad and Mom got a little cocker spaniel named Ginger. Dad came home one day to find that the dog had knocked over a large, free-standing plaster ashtray, breaking it. The dog also chewed up some shoes. In a fit of temper, Dad picked the dog up and threw it across the kitchen. When the dog hit the wall, it fell to the floor and broke its leg. Liking animals, but having a mechanistic view of them, Dad assumed that Ginger's break meant she could not be whole again. So, he decided to put the dog in a sack and drown it in the river. Mom felt mortified when she realized what happened. Ginger was her first dog and Mom loved her. Dad's drowning her seemed unspeakably cruel, and it terrified Mom.

Disorder always pulled Dad out of balance. Children threatened not only physical order, but they also challenged Dad's relationship with Mom. A jealous man by disposition, though cloaking it out of embarrassment, Dad brooked no competition for Mom's attention.

Mom's pressure, however, finally won out. As soon as Dad agreed, Mom got pregnant. The occasion was Gloria and John Farkas' wedding night: February 12, 1950. Dad felt happy when he found out. Mom felt so delighted that the nursery was complete three months in advance of the due date.

In preparation for the birth, Mom quit her job at the E. J. & E. in August when she "started to show." Dad and Grandma Papesh objected. They wanted Mom to take a leave of absence instead of resigning. Grandma volunteered to take care of the baby so Mom could continue to work. Mom's response to Dad was, "Over my dead body! It's my child and I am going to take care of it. Period. And you can tell her so!" The idea of someone else raising her child repelled Mom. Dad reluctantly agreed. He knew better than to fight it when Mom took a dead set stand on something.

LEADING MICKEY HOME

I was born November 25, 1950, the fifth-generation oldest son named Michael, but named after Dad in a shortened version. Dad's middle name was Leopold. Though it was my great grandfather Vesel's full name, neither Mom nor Dad liked it, so they compromised and named me Michael Leo.

My birth, however, was traumatic for Dad. He once said that at three o'clock he had a son, but by six o'clock he had almost lost a wife. Mom began bleeding after my birth, and it went on for some time. Never physically strong, Mom's strength quickly depleted. The bleeding was eventually stanched, and Mom fully recovered, but her recovery took several weeks, and breast-feeding was deemed out of the question. Mom always said that Dad was very good about getting up in the middle of the night to feed me formula so she could sleep and conserve her strength, which helped her heal more quickly. Still, Dad had been quite spooked by the experience.

After a year had passed, Mom began to press Dad for another child, a playmate and companion for me. Dad resisted mightily, now with the additional reason of giving birth's danger to Mom's health. Again, Mom's desires won out. Though the months of Mom's pregnancy coincided with Mom and Dad's labor to open a new funeral home near the time of the due date, Roger's birth November 6, 1952, proceeded without major complications. The doctor knew what to expect.

Mom told the story that I wet my pants when she first brought Roger into the house. She felt surprised since I was already potty trained. "Michael, what happened?" she asked me.

"He makes me nervous," I responded as a twenty-three-month-old.

Other than feeding him a penny in his crib, and Dad having to come in and turn Roger upside down to get the penny out, Roger and I remained close as children. For instance, after he was two or so, I never remember going to bed without his coming to sleep with me at least for a while.

Throughout our childhood, Mom shaped our lives day-to-day. More often than not, Dad was a set of coattails. He made ambulance trips, embalmed for other firms in the area, and managed his own cases at Papesh Funeral Home. Dad rarely played with us. I remember only once being up on his shoulders. Because he couldn't stand it, tickling Dad risked an elbow in the head. We never played catch with Dad or went fishing. We may have been in the backyard pool with Dad once or twice, but he never taught us to swim. Dad was a busy, fleeting figure for us, and a fearsome disciplinarian when Mom felt powerless.

Dad focused on teaching Roger and me how to work. He instructed us carefully about how to sweep and mop the basement: where to begin, where to end, what equipment to use. That instruction ignited my administrative skill. He taught us how to cut the lawn, developing clear expectations about the regularity of the lines when we were done. He instructed us on hedge clipping, car washing, outside window washing, and sash painting. He insisted on basic order in the house so it would always be ready for a stop-in guest. He inspected our work thoroughly and held us accountable.

Twice in our childhood Dad got deeply involved with us in projects that might have been exciting. When I was nine, Dad decided to buy a steel chassis for a little motor car. He made a red plywood floor to place over the chassis and installed a two-horse-power engine. Over the following two summers, he built with us a red and white wood body for the car, liberal with chromium and other discarded car part additions. Dad expected Roger and I to help, and Dad instructed us on how to paint and use tools. Our friends from the neighborhood often came over to help and watch. Occasionally, with Dad on a bike, me driving and Roger sitting beside me, we would tool the neighborhood in the little car. One year we were in the Joliet Halloween parade with it, both of us in costumes. We drove once in the Joliet Christmas parade, too. For that, we spent months building a little float we pulled behind the little car: a Nativity scene on an old wagon.

Ultimately, Roger and I both had mixed reactions to the little car. I liked driving it, but my bookishness left me bored by the work of it. Excellent with tools and stimulated by seeing how things work, Roger enjoyed the building, but felt cheated because he never, ever, drove the little car. We took the car out only with Dad, and he trusted only me to drive.

When I was twelve, Dad decided the car was passé and we ought to have a model train set in the basement. On an old dining room table, we helped Dad build an eight-by-sixteen-foot platform. We placed a tin doll house and barn on it, then painted sidewalks, fields, and roads, trimming the whole of it in green with a little red post-and-dowel fence around the perimeter. We made mountains on it with painted plaster over metal screen, stuffed with newspaper and stapled to a board. Lichen served as bushes and little trees, and all the green areas we coated with paste and sprinkled with green grass. Model airplanes hung on strings from the basement ceiling. Model cars traveled the roads and bridges. Dad procured a huge Hamm's Beer poster from Grandpa's tavern and fastened it to the basement wall behind the set to provide a background scene. By the time the project was over, the board measured twenty by sixteen feet, the trains required two large transformers, the little car had been traded for a passenger train set, and the basement was reduced to a furnace, a laundry station, and a model train yard.

Stimulated by some of the creative aspects of it, I also felt bored by the tedium of the work. Roger seemed essentially to enjoy it. Neither of us, however, spent much time downstairs watching trains go around-and-around, except when our friends came over, dazzled by the whole project.

Dad initiated both projects – the car and the train set – controlled every detail of their design, execution, and ultimate use, and brought them to an end when he decided to do so. Both projects were work, as I experienced them. For all the energy and time they took, and the opportunity to be with Dad they involved, both projects essentially fell flat with Roger and me.

The boxer Dad surprised all of us with one Sunday morning also fell flat with us. Dad never asked us if we wanted a dog, prepared us for the dog's arrival, or engaged us with him in play with the dog. Sparky won a first-place trophy in obedience school, but that was the fruit of Dad's work to bring about household and yard good order. Roger and I mostly cleaned up after Sparky and occasionally walked him. The day Dad gave him away after two years with us, neither Roger nor I, playing in the next yard over, came to say goodbye.

The train set gave way to a pool table in the basement when I was about fifteen. I accepted that. I have no memory of dismantling the train set, which was certainly a massive project. Roger likely carried the burden of that. The pool table, too, like the car, trains, and dog, was Dad's well-intentioned idea of what Rog and I needed and would enjoy with our friends.

As adults, Roger and I shared stories about these four moments in our childhood. At the time, people around us thought we were wonderfully lucky, especially our cousins. In retrospect, Roger and I thought these things, in principle, good experiences for a child. We remembered them fondly and were happy we had the experiences. But given Dad's solitary initiative and work-oriented approach, we ultimately wondered who these things were really for.

•   •   •

"Rog, we were really down the totem pole of Dad's priorities, weren't we?" The sunny Wisconsin countryside and cool morning air offered perfect calm and beauty for reflective conversation.

"Oh, yeah, Mike," he answered with conviction. "His work was always first and Mom second. Then came what he needed to do socially to sustain the business. I am not sure we were even on the list."

"What did he really do for us, then, do you think?" My own answer was inchoate. I always enjoyed Roger's clarity when I was befuddled in my thinking.

"He gave us what he didn't have."

"What do you mean?"

"Education mostly, and material things."

"But he never talked with us about those things, Rog."

"Well, think about it, Mike. Dad gave us an education to the point that he couldn't even talk about it to us. We got so much more than him that we grew beyond him, and he supported that." Roger had a degree in Biology from Loyola in Chicago and was working in quality control at IBM. I had two master's degrees and a doctorate in theological fields.

"No little thing, is it?" I mused.

"No. It was a good thing for him to do. Hard, but a good thing," Roger responded.

Dad and Mom both had sacrificed to get us where we were. Because I had lived away from home since I was sixteen, my sense of what they had given us felt attenuated. Rog, living mostly at home until his mid-twenties, had a far more immediate experience of what we received and what it cost. He certainly named it better.

•   •   •

Roger and I could not have been more divergent in our interests as children. I was neat, tidy, and responsible. I got good grades. Roger was casual to the point of sloppiness and into the fun of things. His grades were middling. I liked to study. When Mom offered to help Rog study, he would burst into tears. I was a goody-goody. Roger rattled the family cage. When friends called to us from outside the back window to come out and play, Roger was always available. If I was reading and enjoying it, I would make excuses. We were very different.

The major category that made the biggest difference in our lives as children was which of us was who's favorite. I was Mom's favorite, it seemed. A more sedentary pair of personalities, Mom and I spent time together talking about relationships, analyzing why people were as they were, and telling family stories. Dad often wanted me to be more active and would nudge Mom to get me outside working on this or that. She would stand in the breach to defend my reading. Dad begrudgingly left me be. I had to toe the mark with Mom, though, and inwardly felt guilty if I veered from her or Dad's expectations.

Roger was Dad's favorite, it seemed. When Dad was home, they putzed together in his workshop. When Dad was gone, Roger could usually be found in the workshop focused on some project or other. Like Dad, he always stayed on the move. Here and there over the years, Dad grew frustrated with Roger's lackadaisical replacement of workshop tools and zany creativity. Several times, Dad threatened to lock up the workroom. Mom always stood in the breach for Rog and preserved his access. With Mom, Rog could smile and hug his way into or out of most anything. At the same time, Mom remarked near the end of her life, "Mike, Roger never knew quite what to do with me."

May 8, 1986, I got an anxious phone call from Mom in Colorado. It was a Thursday evening. Roger and Karen had just had their second child. Karen had felt contractions come upon her suddenly and was rushed to the hospital. By the time Roger got there, she was giving birth by cesarean section to a little boy. When the baby was put into Roger's hands, he immediately realized that something was very wrong. The doctors took the baby from Roger and sped to another room, leaving Rog deeply upset. A few minutes later the doctors told Rog the baby had died. The child had close eyes, no nose, a cleft pallet, and no genitals. It was unusual, the doctors told them, that Karen would not have had a miscarriage at three months. The baby lived only two and one-half minutes. Roger felt shaken. Mom was worried.

I phoned Rog at the hospital in San Jose. Deeply distraught, he told the story, then mused that he didn't know what to say to Karen when she woke up, or what to do about the baby.

I pressed him hard to name the child, to make sure that Karen held the child when she was ready and to plan a funeral for the child when Karen could handle that. We would come. Rog felt unsure. I pressed my points again, hard, attempting to penetrate his grief and confusion.

As I closed the conversation, I asked if he wanted me to call Dad and let him know. He said yes. I hung up and called Dad in Florida.

Feeling upset myself, I told Dad the story. He delivered his response in his casket-side manner. "Thank you, Son, for letting me know. I'll call Roger in a couple of days."

Irritated by his arm's length manner and apparent lack of feeling, especially since Roger was his favorite, I pushed. "Dad, Roger is in pieces. He needs you, Dad," I said very pointedly. "He needs you."

I felt heat as he said firmly and slowly, "I will call Roger in a couple cf days, Son. Probably sometime Saturday."

"Okay, Dad. Whatever you want, Dad," I responded sarcastically. I knew better than to press it further.

I spent the next days concerned for Roger, but decided that, given how hard I had pressed, I should leave him be to make whatever decisions he and Karen wished about the baby. I stewed and stewed about Dad's response, amazed he would respond to Roger as he did. If he cared so little for Roger, what did that mean about his care for me?

That Monday, I had an appointment with my spiritual director. I told him the whole story and my response to Dad.

"Mike," he said. "For many years you have thought that your father had given Roger something that he had not given you. Mike, he hasn't given it to Roger, either. He withheld feelings from both of you, not just you. Both of you."

The idea amazed me. Could it be?

Later that day I called Roger. I told him what had happened with Dad and what my spiritual director had said about it.

"Oh, yeah, Mike, that's right."

"What?" I felt shocked. "But you were his favorite. You spent all that time together when we were little."

"Yeah, Mike, but there was nothing there."

Surprised still, I had to press the point. "What did the two of you talk about in all those hours together?"

"O-o-o-h, putzing," Rog said matter-of-factly. "That's all."

"Putzing!" I reacted. "Rog, aside from a sheer sense of duty, why would you go down to Florida today to visit Dad?"

"Oh, I would go down if I had learned something that I thought he ought to know, or if he learned something that I wanted to know in the area of putzing. That would be good for a three- or four-day Florida visit, I suppose."

"Really!" His taking this perspective for granted caught me off guard. His giving subject matter priority over warm feeling, which he evidently lacked, undercut my age-old conception of Dad's loving Roger more and me less.

"Rog, beyond duty, why would I go down to visit Dad in Florida?" We were talking in narrow, practical terms, but I wanted to understand his perspective.

"Well, I suppose you could talk about your being a priest, and funerals and stuff like that. That's what you have in common."

"Rog, those conversations would fill the time for only about a day."

"Then, Mike, that's all you should stay!" Roger chirped back.

When I asked him if Dad had called, Rog said he had. Saturday. "Actually, his conversation was the most helpful, Mike. He had no feelings at all. He put his funeral director's hat on and laid out all the options for me. It helped."

Rog and Karen decided that we would have a funeral for the child they had named Charley. Mom and I went. Rog decided not to tell Dad they were going to have the funeral. Rog concluded that Dad certainly wouldn't come, and it wouldn't have mattered to him.

The whole event marked a turning point for me in my understanding of my relationship with Dad, and his with Roger.

When we were four and two, Dad characterized our unique personalities as "the professor" and "the clown." One significant symbol of the difference between us was that I was always called Michael or Michael Leo. Only Roger called me Mike. Dad and Mom usually called Roger either Rogie, or Charlie, or Chuckie Boy, affectionate diminutives.

In seminary high school and college from 1964, I wore a coat and tie most every day. I refrained from drinking much, usually went to bed around nine-thirty - even in college - and was sneaky enough to confine my antics to the boarding school context without getting caught. Two years behind me, Roger had friends, did drugs, and had sex, long hair, and fast cars, coupled with a belligerent attitude, right under Mom and Dad's noses. We all bore the consequences of Roger's and my unwavering patterns.

In 1990 I received my doctoral degree. By that time in our lives, I felt frustrated enough with Dad's behavior to want to use the commencement ceremony as an excuse to have a summit among him, Rog, and me. Roger agreed. We decided we wanted to talk through our expectations regarding Christmas, Easter, birthdays, and visits. Dad had been passive-aggressively indicating his displeasure with our lack of attention to him even as he was, at best, hit and miss with his attention to us and Roger's two children.

The idea of coming for the graduation appealed to Dad, and he seemed to like the fact the three of us would be together. He never mentioned Lil's coming at all, which surprised Roger and I and affirmed our idea of making our get-together a summit, though we said nothing about that to Dad.

Roger and Dad arrived separately on a Friday afternoon. Graduation was Sunday with a party to follow. We spent Saturday together, interrupted only by my celebrating Mass. We spent the most significant time Saturday afternoon sitting in Dad's and Roger's guest room in the seminary where I worked. We swapped stories about times past.

With Roger laying back on his bed with a glassy "I feel naked" look in his eye, Dad sat in a chair across the room and spoke of how difficult Roger had been to raise. Dad stated that I was always good, easy to handle. Roger, on the other hand, had created enormous stress between Mom and him, and Dad still felt angry about it. He flushed when he spoke about Roger's teen years and used blunt, explicit language, reporting what happened then and what he thought about it.

Rog and I later agreed that, at sixty-five years of age, a decade and more after the events, Dad still sounded bitter. While I thought Dad unfair, I had been boarding at school most of those years and had little response to make beyond my attentiveness and inner surprise. I felt bad for Rog.

Dad spilled about other things, too. He expressed his disillusionment about our abandoning him and Mom in the 1970s at the time of their divorce, our lack of communication with him, and our failure to treat Lil and her daughters with the deference – exaggerated and inappropriate in our view – that he wished. Dad clearly expected that we would all be one happy family, even though we traveled to Florida solely at our own initiative. Dad and Lil never invited either of us to share a holiday with them and rarely visited us. They offered only hit-and-miss acknowledgment of birthdays and holidays.

With Dad's expectations up and out, I decided to move in to get to the point of the visit. I was the son gifted with Dad's Slovenian directness. "Dad, do you expect us to acknowledge your birthday?"

"Yes, Son, I do."

"Do you want a card? A gift?"

"A card would be fine."

"Dad, I would like a card on my birthday, too," I stated. He shifted awkwardly.

"I would like that, too, Dad, and for Michael and Kristen, maybe even Karen."

"Oh. Okay, Son." Dad squirmed.

"Dad," I asked, "would you like a card at Christmas, or a card and gift?"

"I think a card would be fine." I knew he had some money problems, but Christmas was Christmas.

"Dad, how about a card and a gift, from me to you and you to me. Is that okay?"

"Okay." He seemed deflated, unsure.

"And, Dad, how about us, too?" Roger chimed in. "You don't have to give much. But my children don't really know their Papesh grandparents. It would help if you sent them at least something. We would do the same."

For the second and last time ever, Dad visited Roger and his family during the summer of 1989. He and then six-year-old Michael were both early risers, so they met together in the kitchen for breakfast on the first day. Dad told me later that when they sat down at the breakfast table Michael opened a discussion. "Grandpa Papesh, how are you related to us?"

"I am your father's father, Michael." I heard Dad's hurt in his voice as he told the story.

"Does that mean you are Uncle Mike's father, too?"

"Yes, Michael. I am his father, too."

"And you used to be married to Grandma Arado?" I imagined Dad felt stunned by that question and Michael's ability to pull things together.

"Yes."

"Oh, okay, now I get it," Michael said.

Dad sounded almost teary in the telling.

Dad seemed to feel especially vulnerable around what Roger had said in our summit. He agreed to send a card and gifts.

"How about calls, Dad? Is once a month enough?" I was starting to feel more at ease, and more assertive as a result. Dad seemed fine with what was happening.

"I think once a month is fine."

"And what about visits, Dad? What do you expect? Is once a year about right?" I asked. It never occurred to me to ask if he would recip-rocate visits, just as I let go asking about his calling us by phone. Both were beyond his expectations and mine by that time.

Though the weekend continued, and we had a pleasant time to-gether with no evidence of strain, the summit element of the visit ended with the grilling. Roger and I both thought the summit was worth it and sensed that Dad got the message that the street was more than one way, if not quite fully two-ways. The clarity helped both of us. We hoped it would help Dad. We assumed Lil would agree with whatever he decided.

In the car together after taking Dad to the airport Sunday evening, Roger and I talked. "Did you notice that Dad has only two emotions, Rog?" I asked.

"Yeah, anxiety and anger. Oh, he probably has sexual feelings too, lots of them!" We chuckled.

"He also laughs, so that makes four. But there's not much else, is there?" I rejoined.

"No," Rog said. "Isn't that sad."

•　　•　　•

"Rog," I asked as we drove down Wisconsin, "do you think Dad liked us?"

"I don't know, Mike. I suppose so, sort of. I think he was so busy partying around Florida with Lil that we didn't really matter much. He was doing what he wanted to do and that's all he cared about."

"Did you like him?" I asked.

"Yeah, he was okay. We didn't have much in common. It was probably worse for you."

"Yeah, it was. Our interests overlapped almost not-at-all. When I would call, we didn't really have much to talk about. During the three or four years before he went into the nursing home, though, I appreciated his being able to say that he loved me. I am also grateful I was able to say it back."

"That was nice, wasn't it?" Rog said matter-of-factly. "I am not sure what I meant by it," Rog went on, "but it was nice to be able to say it."

We met Mom and Joe at the Sun Prairie A&W as planned. When we got there, they were already eating. We joined them for hot dogs and root beer, talking lightly about the road mostly. As we left, we agreed to switch partners. Mom rode with me.

CHAPTER VIII
To Illinois with Mom

"Well, Mike, how was the ride with Roger?" Mom dove right in as always. Often, that helped. Occasionally, it didn't.

"We had a wonderful conversation. I enjoyed being with him very much. We talked about all sorts of stuff. I think he's generally doing pretty well." Then I added meaningfully, with a glint of trouble in my eye I am sure, "And now I get to find out what's cooking with you."

Mom chuckled. She was always ready to talk.

"How are you?" I asked.

"I'm fine. Your dad's death is no different for me than anyone else's, really. I have no strong feelings one way or the other. I feel sad for him and I pray for him but that's about it."

"Does Dad's death bring up all kinds of stuff?"

"Not really. I just feel sorry for him that his whole life was about sex, money, and the funeral business."

"What do you mean by that?" I thought I understood but her summary had been rather stark.

"Well, all he wanted from me was sex."

"Was that true your whole life together?"

"Well, not at first. When we kissed at Troppe's that first time he folded his lips under his teeth like this." She mimicked the gesture. We laughed. "He didn't know anything. Of course, neither did I. Before he left for the service it started but the service changed him."

"How?"

"Well he never even kissed me the whole first year we dated. When he had his appendix out at sixteen, he asked me to come to the hospital and he gave me a ring. I stopped in the chapel on the way out and asked God to help me like him. My mother liked him, though. He dressed like a million bucks, was very polite and he was rather sissified. She thought I would be safe. I was for a while." Then, turning meaningfully toward me, she said, "Until he found out how safe cemeteries could be."

"Mother!" I exclaimed in mock shock.

"Well, Mike, it's true. But during his time in the service I think he saw lots."

•   •   •   •

Dad talked about his Word War II service maybe twice when we were little. He told fun stories about cutting rats' tails in the South Pacific as they ran over the net above their heads. He mentioned that they carried enough baseball equipment with them for a whole team. He had been among the troops in Tokyo with General MacArthur and saw him once. These stories were about it. I saw pictures, mostly showing Dad with a friend named Mac. These marked a time in Dad's life, but he said nothing about them. I knew from Mom that they wrote to each other every day. I concluded from the stories and the silence that Dad disliked the army, stayed focused on Mom States-side, felt glad to get out and that it meant very little to him.

When he was seventy-two, about mid-way through his Alzheimer's degeneration, I was down in Florida visiting. I asked him what he remembered about the service. He spoke about shipping into Tokyo Bay and seeing charred corpses hanging on the rigging of burned-out hulks of ships. His attention span very brief, he passed onto something else almost immediately. It was then that I realized that his World War II experience was deeply buried somewhere within, something he was incapable of bringing up or even reflecting upon, but it hurt. Maybe PTSD hurt.

•   •   •

"He was different when he came back," Mom went on. "He was more defiant or something."

"What did that have to do with sex?" I probed.

"Well, he expected it. He came back in April and we married right away in November 1946. We were too young. He was twenty-one and I was twenty."

•   •   •

Dad and Mom entered an international marriage by Joliet, Illinois standards. When they decided to marry in 1946, Grandma and Grandpa Papesh wanted to know, "Mickey, why can't you find a nice Slovenian girl?"

Aunt Nell asked, "Mary Jean, wherever did you meet a foreigner like that?"

Dad and Mom had gone steady since 1942, spending more and more time together, and with each other's families, especially the Papeshes on Ruby St. This continued after Mom began at "the J" in March 1943 until Dad was signed up for the Army Air Corps in January 1944.

Dad began his military service that February. He tried to make it in the Army Airways Communications Center but failed the test. So, he went to the Army base at Rantoul, Illinois, for training, then to Salt Lake City, and finally to Boca Raton, Florida, before being shipped out to Mindanao and Japan in late 1944.

Though Dad and Mom wrote every day, they also continued to date other people a little. In one of her letters, Mom asked Dad if he ever dated. He wrote back that he had gone out with someone in Salt Lake City. Since he had dated, Mom decided she could, too. Each dated rarely, though, and continued to write each other daily.

Dad gave Mom an engagement ring in December 1944 at Boca Raton, Florida. Her father procured two railroad passes to take Mom to Florida to visit Dad. Dad's folks came to the train station to see them off. Mom had no idea at the time that the Papeshes had bought her a diamond, and that they had come to the train expressly to pass it to her father. Suspecting nothing, Mom missed Grandpa passing the ring to her father, and she also missed her father passing the ring to Dad. So, in Florida, oceanside at Del Rey Beach where they were staying, Dad proposed, and Mom accepted.

Throughout the rest of his service time, Dad worked to save the bulk of his army salary for his and Mom's future. Mom spent some of her time with Dad's family, saved money and readied herself to be married when Mickey returned.

Dad was twenty years old when he came home from the service. Grandpa Papesh wanted to send Dad to Notre Dame to get a college education. Dad was clear, however, that he wanted to go to Worsham College of Mortuary Science. He had decided, while in the service, to become a funeral director. Dad had been raised just across the street from Racki's small funeral home. He also remembered the old Slovenian funeral director cattycorner across from St. Joe's church, who cut a fine figure, wore a white suit, and who knew great respect in the Slovenian community. He wanted the look and the respect. Unmotivated toward study, however, Dad also knew that becoming a funeral director and mortician took only nine months of school and two years of apprenticeship rather than four full years. Inclined both to Grandpa's commitment to hours of work and Grandma's preference for being at home, Dad also thought funeral directing would be convenient – ideal in fact – for living above your business. That way, he thought, he could be at work downstairs while always available to home and family up-stairs. Becoming a funeral director was Dad's dream.

During the summer of 1946, Dad asked a customer of Grandpa's, a Mr. Schupe, for a construction job. Though he was living at the Papesh family homestead, Dad wanted to be independent from Grandpa and earn better money than he could at the tavern. Mr. Schupe gave him a job, assigning him to help pave streets.

Grandpa was furious that Dad had asked for the job without telling him, that Schupe had given Dad the job, and that his son was "out in the public" working as a "common laborer." He felt so mad, in fact, that he refused to acknowledge Dad's presence when he drove by the work sites. Dad made good money, though, and saved it. He entered Worsham College that September.

Coming to agreement about wedding plans underlined the great differences between Dad's and Mom's families and set the pattern of relationship between them. The Irish family wanted a small cake and punch reception at a hotel. They could comfortably afford that and thought it suitable. The Papeshes wanted a big hall wedding with the St. Joe's parish women cooking and serving a meal, and Fred Troppe's band playing polkas for a wedding dance. Grandpa wanted a bar as well, of course. The Irish family saw the wedding as a small family affair. The Slovenian family saw it as a business opportunity. Except for the selection of the church and priest, the Slovenians had their way. The Irish groused among themselves, however, and failed to be won over.

Mom and Dad married on November 28, 1946. It was a cold Thanksgiving Day. The church seemed full. In a wedding party of eight, Dad's closest friend, Clare Lesser, was best man and Mom's sister, fifteen-year-old Joanie, was maid of honor. Grandpa Papesh sobbed openly in the front pew. Losing "Sonny," he couldn't contain himself. Mom and the whole Irish family felt insulted at his display, and so did Mom's French Canadian and English father.

After the wedding, the close family and wedding party breakfasted at St. Joe's Hall downtown. The family then went to their homes for a brief rest before going to the St. Joe's Park hall at four o'clock for the reception, dinner, and dance. With a bar every few feet around the hall, booze flowed. Troppe's One Man Kitchen Band played polkas all night.

The whole affair stunned the Irish family, convincing them of the high value of "marrying Irish." Mom simply felt worn out by the whole experience. As for the Slovenian family, people talked about the reception for years. Though Mom and Dad left at ten o'clock for their honeymoon, the party went on and on. It was good for business. Grandpa Papesh paid for everything.

In the pictures of the wedding day, Dad looks long and gangly in a mourning coat. Mom's eyes are half-closed. She says she was having her period; Grandma couldn't believe Mom's naiveté. Mom's explanation, "We talked about absolutely everything in our family except sex. We never talked about that." The rest of the pictures suggest everyone else's joy.

Dad and Mom honeymooned one night at the Palmer House in Chicago. They had to get back to move into an apartment that weekend and get ready for work on Monday. In my late teens I found a record Dad made in the honeymoon suite before they went to bed. He sang, *I Love You So Much It Hurts Me* and then said he adored Mom. Dad was in a swoon over Mom, but not Mom with him, she said with characteristic matter-of-factness.

At the time of their wedding, Dad and Mom had relatively few resources for gaining clarity about love and covenant relationship. They certainly thought they were in love, though. They were also two good people looking for escape from their family circumstances, honest support in a faithful and loving relationship, and genuine security for their future. Their fundamental values were solid and in some harmony. There was reason for hope.

• • •

"During the first years of our marriage," Mom went on, "I would be working all day at 'the J,' and I would come home tired and having to fix dinner. He expected sex. It got worse after you were born, worse still after Roger was born. After I got my thyroid problem taken care of, he felt free to demand whatever he wanted."

"Was it mutual?" I was interested but unsure about boundaries. I knew I had a right not to know some things.

"No," she said dismissively. "He would say, 'It's going to be tonight, so be ready,' and I had to be ready. When you two were in school he would say, 'I'll be home for lunch, so be ready.' There was never anything natural about it for me. It was as if sex released some kind of tension in him or something, and I was the dupe."

"You sound offended by it all."

"I was," she said emphatically. "This happened several times a week. Then there was, 'Wear this nightgown,' and, 'Wear those high heels.' It was awful. I hated it."

"Did he know?"

"Well, I was one hell of an actress. I played the game. But he probably knew. It didn't matter to him, though. His needs were first, and that was it."

"He was completely self-preoccupied," I dared to hazard.

"Totally." I could hear the exasperation in her voice. "He was all that mattered, not me. Not you and Roger, either. That was true with money, too."

"How do you mean?" True to her Irish heritage, Mom clung to her resentments. I allowed her to vent, and she liked that. No one else really did. Sometimes I listened passively and felt beat-up by what she shared. Today I was strong, detached, interested.

"We-e-e-e-ll, he spent money like it was water. He never consulted me about anything. He just spent. I had the checkbook and had to live with the bills every month. He couldn't handle money at all."

•   •   •

Dad saved $2,000 during his two years in the Army Air Corps. When he came home, he had trouble deciding if he wanted to buy a car or get married. Mom insisted that she had waited long enough for him, and now it was time to get married. However, Dad spent the $2,000 for furniture: a claret-red mohair couch and side chair, a gold lounge chair, pea green carpet, lamps, and mahogany end, tier, and coffee tables. This spending opened up money as a specter in their relationship.

Mom worked at the E. J. & E., providing living for them both while Dad attended Worsham College of Mortuary Science. When school was over, Dad began his apprenticeship at a Joliet funeral home making $25 per week. Dad and Mom still owed $300 on their furniture, which Grandpa Papesh paid off at Christmas of 1946 as a gift. Mom felt greatly relieved.

They saved $600 during their first year of marriage, but then Dad received $900 from the GI Bill for his Worsham tuition. He decided to spend it on a green 1948 Ford coupe. They had no car and Dad had confessed that he yearned for the day that Mom would be able to drive and not have to walk everywhere. Shocked by the idea of owning a new car, Mom argued with Dad about it. Grandpa Papesh thought the expenditure reckless.

Then in early 1948, a few months after the Ford was purchased, Mom made her argument again, and Grandpa blew his top when Dad traded the Ford in for a 1947 Chrysler seven-passenger limousine. The limousine had a removable front seat and side bar at the right-side passenger doors so that a cot could be placed in the car to make an ambulance out of it. The trade was unequal, so Dad also took on car payments.

At this same time, Mom and Dad also moved from their one-bedroom to a two-bedroom apartment. Their financial situation grew more complicated in 1949 when Dad quit his apprenticeship job because the owner's wife accused him of stealing toilet paper. An honest man, he could not bear the insult.

In a financial pickle, Dad asked Grandpa if he could work at the tavern part time. Grandpa agreed, hoping to pound some sense into Dad, I suspect. Dad made $50 per week. He also did some ambulance work on the side with the Chrysler, which earned him three dollars per trip. Most of the day, however, Dad was home alone, planning for a new funeral home of his own. Mom says he talked all the time about nothing else.

Still short on cash, living off Mom's salary mainly, Dad decided to buy a console radio for $100 so he could have music during the day as he planned. Then he borrowed $2,000 from Mom's Aunt Nell for the architectural plans of a funeral home. When he presented the plans to the city planning commission, his best friend's parents appeared against him because they did not want a funeral home in the neighborhood. "So, the whole thing died," Mom said. "Money out the window!"

In 1952, still making ambulance trips on the side and working part time at the tavern, Dad heard that the owner of one of the two Slovenian funeral homes was trying to sell the business. Anton Nemanich had died in 1946 and his widow, Marie, who had enough on her hands with the floral business next door to the funeral home, wanted out. Though the funeral home had had only seven funerals the previous year, she wanted $6,000 up front for the business, plus monthly rent of $150 for the building. Dad just had to have it, so he went down to Henry Hammel and borrowed the money. Grandpa, having learned hard lessons about partnership with Hammel, hit the roof again. Defiant, Dad set about cleaning up the place and buying used furniture. Then, when the Funeral Directors Association informed him that he had to have a hearse or he could not open, Grandpa took on the expense because Dad had traveled far down the path toward opening the business and had no money to buy a hearse.

By August 1952, Dad had the likely fulfillment of his dreams in place. He had a hearse and limousine, he operated an ambulance business and a free-lance embalming business, and he had his own Papesh Funeral Home. He was also buried in debt to a car dealership, Aunt Nell, Henry Hammel, Grandpa Papesh, and the landlords of the apartment and funeral home buildings. Though Mom felt deeply anxious, and Grandpa was mad, Dad remained calm about it all. His philosophy was that debt was simply part of owning your own business. He worked hard and felt happy.

Mom felt burdened by enormous stress when it came to money because Dad's spending habits frustrated her. She processed all the bills and cash flow remained always a problem. They only had enough money each month to pay a few dollars on each bill. Eventually the Papesh Funeral Home cash flow stress became too much for Mom and she refused to have anything to do with the funeral home accounting. Years later she offered this uncharacteristically sharp critique: "That dead horse! It was a dump with some sticks of furniture in it when we bought it and it was still a dump when we opened it!"

•　　•　　•

"The pattern continued through our whole marriage, Mike. He borrowed from my mother, too. I told him I wouldn't get involved in that, or with Nell, so he had to talk to them himself."

"I bet Grandma made it tough." She was, in her own words, tighter than the skin on a peach.

"You bet. When he asked her, she said, 'I don't see any reason why I should be deprived of interest because you need some money. I'll give you the money, but you'll have to pay me the same interest the bank would.'"

"That was okay with him?" I asked.

"Sure. He needed the money. Ernie Wunderlich was even worse." Dad called Ernie his best friend his whole life. Nearly twenty years older than Dad and quite enterprising financially, Ernie served more as mentor than friend.

"What did he do?"

"He told your father, 'Michael, I won't lend you any money. But I'll tell you what I will do. If you need money, I would be willing to co-sign a loan at the bank for you.'"

"Did Dad do it?"

"No. Frankly, it was too risky for him."

I found it hard to comprehend the financial straitjacket Dad had so willingly donned. "Did he climb out of the rut he was in?"

"To some extent. When he sold the funeral home in 1964 to go with Dames, he found $4,800 in the business checkbook he didn't know he had. He couldn't add! He also got some good money for the funeral home furniture he sold. He paid back his father and my mother at that time. It was too late for his father; the tavern was too far gone. And he never paid Nell back at all. She was eighty-nine and in a nursing home."

"And the pattern continued?"

"You bet! Big cars, furniture, trips – which were all about sex – you name it. I fought the house on Glenwood all the way, as you know. Nope. It had to be his way. He had to impress people. That was it."

"You got fed up?"

"Oh, yeah, Mike. I wanted security and there was no security with him."

"Financial security?"

"Yes. When Roger was about to start college, I asked your dad how we would pay for the first year. He said, 'Well, I guess we'll have to borrow money.' 'What about the next year?' I asked. 'We'll just have to borrow that, too.' 'And the next year and the next?' 'We'll borrow that, too.'" Mom sighed. "There was no end in sight, Mike. I got completely fed up."

"That was the reason you left him?"

"It was several things. All he did was work, and when he didn't work, he wanted sex. I got sick and tired of the sex thing. I was never much on that anyway. Then he was spending money we didn't have. I lost respect for him totally. By the time I left him I had no feelings for him at all."

"None?"

"None. He tried to be a nice person, I suppose, but I was sick and tired of what I had to put up with. We kept a happy face on it, but I wasn't happy. When we were about to celebrate our twenty-fifth anniversary, we were out with Svetiches. They had just had theirs and Marg talked about how wonderful it was. I thought to myself, 'What's that about? Are you kidding? Not with what I have to put up with.' I really didn't want to hurt him, though. That's why I only took $15,000 at the divorce, and that for Roger's education. He didn't care about Roger's education, and Roger was going to get a college degree no matter what it cost as far as I was concerned. I told Joe there was nothing else, only the house, really. Your dad had worked hard. I thought he should keep what he had worked so hard for. If I had known he would remarry and take so little care of his children, and be so resentful, I would have taken more."

"The spiritual tradition teaches, Mom, that self-knowledge, honesty with one's self, is critical to growth. I don't think Dad was an especially honest person within himself. I don't think he got it."

"You're probably right. But the thing I never could understand was why he was mad at me all those years after I left. I always supported him. I studied with him every day when he went to Worsham. I took care of the bills. I worked. I did the little act he had to have so badly. I don't know why he was mad at me. Didn't he realize that eventually I would get sick-and-tired of it all and get out? Anyone would."

"That's my point, Mom. I don't think that he had a very firm grasp of reality. When push came to shove, I don't think Dad knew what he really thought and felt about anything. Didn't one of Roger's girlfriends hit the nail on the head when she said he was all front and no back?"

"Boy, did she ever," Mom said with certainty. "That was Aurora."

"I have often wondered if life for Dad wasn't, essentially, a picture in his head that he tried to follow and live up to," I mused. "Once you

126

left, you didn't fit the picture. Roger and I didn't fit the picture. His only alternative was resentment. Hell, I am not sure even Lil fit the picture."

"I think you're right about that," she said. She paused for a moment, and then picked up on the Lil end of the remark. "That whole bowling crowd knew Lil's reputation. All the Slovenians knew that she was sleeping around and had been for years. There probably came a time when he realized that."

"And so, he moved to Florida."

"You know, I never thought about that," Mom responded, making connections from what I could guess.

"Me neither."

"He moved to Florida because of what happened at Dames' and, of course, he had to save face. But he could have moved to Florida because he really couldn't live with Lil in Joliet. They all knew."

"Hmmmmm. Could be." I needed time to think about that.

"You know, Michael, I think all this had to do with the Alzheimer's, too. I think that for years he probably suffered from depression, and depression is connected with Alzheimer's. I thought the same of your Grandmother Papesh, too. So much of her life fell apart."

"I know. I thought that of Grandma, too. It seemed that her falling into mumbling silence was the only way she could ultimately deal with life. The same may have been true for Dad."

"I think it was. Everything was about success and he had so many failures."

The three hours with Mom flew by. We drove right to the hotel in Joliet. Roger and Joe beat us by a few minutes. We checked in and cleaned up. I decided to wait to call Lil and Gloria until after supper. We ate at our favorite restaurant, a Slovenian place famous in town for a sandwich called "the poor boy," cube steak on a hard roll smothered with garlic butter. "Rich boy" should have been its name. After supper we drove around town. We had not seen Joliet together for many years and I was the one who had been there most recently, three years before. We found the new Fred C. Dames Funeral Home, which was a straight shot from the hotel. Gloria's place was in between. Our meandering took us by many old haunts, including St. Joe's cemetery. Dad's grave was already dug and covered with planks. I felt sobered when I saw it.

We arrived back at the hotel about eight o'clock. I called Lil at Lynn's to tell her we were in town. She asked how our trip was and mentioned she would be seeing Dad tomorrow morning but said nothing about our getting together before three-thirty, right before the wake. I was content with those plans, even preferred them.

I called Gloria. She asked about when we got in and the trip, but also suggested nothing. She did have a piece of news, though. "Michael, I need to tell you that I talked with Marge Raker today, and she will be coming to the wake."

"Oh, how nice." Marge was the daughter of Grandpa Papesh's sister Antonia.

"Well, I'm not so sure. She asked if you were coming. She wanted to see you. I think she has something to say."

Four years earlier, I had done a brief sketch of family history for the Papeshes based on research I had done in Slovenia in 1991 and in the Will County Courthouse in Joliet. Among many other things, the research turned up information I had not known about Great-Aunt Antonia's birth. I sent the summary to Gloria to see what she thought. To my surprise she sent it to cousins. Though I had never met Marge, I gathered she had some concerns. "Oh, dear. Well, thanks for the warning."

"I just wanted to let you know." I could hear a little titillation in Gloria's voice. She loved trouble. Always had.

"O-o-o-o-okay!" I said.

"I'll see you tomorrow. About three-thirty?" Gloria asked.

"Right. Rog and I will be there."

Again, though surprised, I was content that there would be no getting together with Gloria and her family much before the beginning of the wake. Especially given Mom's presence, waiting until three-thirty presented less risk. Besides, Gloria might be inclined to ask if Mom knew Dad died and what she thought. I preferred avoiding the subject, if I could, and needed time to prepare myself internally.

I went into the adjacent room and reported to Mom, Joe, and Rog. "Well, I talked with Lil and Gloria. I guess we're free until the wake begins."

"Oh, that's great," Mom said.

"You are going to see George Klepec at St. Joe's in the morning, then?" Rog asked.

"The appointment is scheduled for a quarter after nine. I was hoping you would come along." I knew he would want to. Going to St. Joe's would be nostalgic, and I thought Roger would enjoy it. Far more sentimental than me, Rog was little inclined to show it.

"Oh, sure," he said. "I've got nothing else better to do."

"How long will that take?" Mom asked.

"I'm not sure. We should probably leave the bulk of the morning for whatever happens there. We should be back before eleven o'clock."

"We can go to lunch after, then go to the funeral home." Mom compulsively planned.

"Now, how will that work?" Joe asked. He was wary, concerned.

"Well, Lil will be there in the morning…" I began.

"…and it will take her the whole afternoon just get her hair done and her dress on," Rog continued. "No problem for us. We have all afternoon!" He said with his hands in the air and a laugh.

"Right," I said. "So, we can go at one o'clock or so, after lunch. Jeff Dames told me that any time after one o'clock would be okay."

"Then we will have breakfast together?" Mom asked.

"Yes. That would be nice."

"When?" she asked.

"How about eight o'clock?"

"Sounds like a plan," Joe said, and we retired to our rooms.

As we laid down to sleep, I asked Roger across the room how he was doing.

"Oh, fine," he said. "It's a funny kind of time. I'm not sure what to make of it."

"Me neither. My only concern is that Mom and Joe's being here won't interfere with whatever it is that's supposed to happen around Dad."

"Right. I think it will be okay."

"Do you feel sad at all, Rog?"

"I feel sad for Dad, but not lots of anything else, really. How about you?"

"Me neither. I am wondering when grief will come."

"Who knows! I guess we'll just have to find out!"

CHAPTER IX
Returning to Slovenski Rim

Tuesday morning at six o'clock, I went out for a solitary walk in over-hot drizzle – partly because I couldn't sleep, partly to create some emotional space for whatever was to come that day, partly for exercise, partly because I needed time to pray. I enjoyed this time of day most. My feelings bubbled up then, and I felt free to talk and pray through what was really going on deep inside. That morning I felt anxious about what Dad's corpse would look like, and about my encounters with the family at the funeral home. I had always felt somewhat disconnected from Gloria's family, as well as from Lil. I wanted that to recede that day. I also felt a little afraid that Mom and Joe's being on hand might be too noisy emotionally, creating nervous anxiety that would get in the way of my being hospitable to the family and to whomever would come to the wake. The walk helped me calm and let go of my anxieties.

When I returned to the hotel room Roger was up and chatting with Mom and Joe in their room. I showered and dressed for breakfast. Rog followed right away, and we arrived downstairs for breakfast by a quarter to eight. I usually ate a continental breakfast, and the motel had everything on hand, muffins substituting for bread. I got Diet Coke from a nearby machine. The four of us chatted lightly about the day, reaffirming our plans. We agreed that we would eat lunch at eleven-thirty.

After breakfast and tooth brushing for me and a cigarette for Rog, we drove to St. Joe's for our appointment. When we arrived, the secretary ushered us into George Klepec's office, where he sat with a veiled woman who turned out to be his sister. George looked as I remembered him. Of medium height, his reddish-brown hair had only a hint of gray, which belied his sixty years. Rather than the combed and parted style of times past, though, his hair was all combed forward, a light version of Moe Howard. I gathered he was hiding something. He had a strong jaw and large chin, a clear, fair complexion, and an ever-present, wide smile that revealed short, straight teeth. Dressed in casual clerical blacks with gum shoes, he walked with a slight limp. His glasses, though different from the clear-brown plastic horn rims I remembered from years ago, seemed to complete his face, adding a reflective air.

He invited us to talk in the kitchen. As I walked through the rectory, I noted fluorescent lights in all the rooms, including what used to be the dining room. I sensed that George might be one of those brisk-mannered managers, both forceful and easy-going, unrepentantly negligent about details, oblivious to thoughtful touches in his relationships, but a talker delighting in stories about the characters he had met and endlessly available to serve his people. His five cups of coffee in our hour-and-a-quarter kitchen conversation underlined my impression that he needed to keep talking and moving in order to remain peaceful inside.

His sister, the sister, appeared to be an older, shorter, thinner version of George with a jutting chin, her hair straight back from her forehead in a pageboy. She, however, seemed more tranquil. She drank but one cup of coffee. I was amused to note that, though they were obviously very close, they called each other exclusively "Father George" and "Sister." His kissing her goodbye later during our visit seemed ill-fitting, yet utterly incidental. They were Catholic traditionalists, but family.

George ushered Roger and I into the rectory kitchen, a small, bright, bare place with old white appliances and a white floor, a medium-sized maple table and chairs, and dark cabinets. I saw no effort to coordinate anything; it looked like a dumping ground. It was, we found out later. George lived elsewhere. We sat at the cluttered kitchen table and were offered coffee each of the five times George got up to pour a cup for himself. Roger had one cup and a warm-up. I drank water.

Other than a brief time during which we talked through the particulars of the funeral ritual, which I was led to believe George and I executed essentially the same way, Father George and Sister told stories of people they had known in previous assignments. Sister also talked about her house of prayer ministry for her order. Their hospitality was classically Slovenian, warm, gracious, and roundabout. George discreetly snuck in spontaneous direct questions – his real concerns – amid a flurry of incidental remarks and amusing stories about people and their interrelationships. I could see rather quickly that we really had little to talk through. Rather, Roger and I were being weighed and assessed, though most kindly, because we lived away from home. They, and we, assumed we belonged together. We had all been baptized in the same font, raised in the same town and parish, and belonged to the same tribe. George and Sister aimed to glean if we understood that and how we fit.

●   ●   ●

In the sixth century, one Slavic tribe settled in the chicken-shaped area of Central Europe bordered by the Julian Alps on the north, the Kamnik Mountains on the south, the Adriatic on the east and the Hungarian plain on the west. The Slovenes, ruled by an elected chief who made pronouncements in tribal gatherings from a rock near what is now Klagenfurt, Austria, were conquered by the Franks in 743, then afterward the Germans, then by the Austro-Hungarian Empire. Though serfs for the ruling class, the Slovenes preserved their language, customs, and identity thanks to the ministry of the native Roman Catholic priests.

In the late nineteenth century, because of upheaval within the Austro-Hungarian Empire, some Slovenes migrated to the United States. In my family, the migrants were the Papesh and Vesel families.

The Papesh family – *papez* means *pope* in Slovenian – came to the United States in the early to mid-1890s. They were rooted in Grosuplje, a mountainous area of Slovenia southeast of Ljublanja, the capital, near the mouth of the Krka River. Both Michael Martin Papesh and his wife, Mary Perko, came from a tiny village, Korinj, split up-and-down the side of a mountain. The double village joined at a little public oratory dedicated to St. George. The mountain peak had been an ancient Roman lookout post on the Via Postumia to Asia Minor. A church had stood there since the fourth century. The village comprised two small clusters of six or seven houses, one up the hill and one down, with barns adjacent. The farmland, about an acre for each family, fanned out from the villages. The Papesh family lived in the lower village, the Perko family in the upper. The families were deeply inbred. My great-great-grandparents, John Perko and Agatha Meglan, for instance, were raised next door to each other. Each house had a separate name, and the house name determined how the families were ordered in the parish registry at a village five miles distant named Krka.

Born in 1868, Mary Perko bore a child out of wedlock in 1889, whom she named Mary Catherine. No word came down through the family about Aunt Mary's paternity. In July 1893, leaving little Mary Catherine behind, Mary Perko came to the United States and settled in the Slovenian community at Joliet, Illinois. Slovenian emigration to the United States was lively in the 1890s and Slovenians from nearby villages had already sent family to Joliet to work in the mills. It tempts the imagination to think that Mary's emigrating to the United States served as a way for the pious, Catholic Perko's to escape some of the shame wrought by Mary's having a baby out of wedlock.

In July 1894, Mary Perko became pregnant again. We know nothing about the circumstances of the pregnancy. Because of the high likelihood that she supported herself doing housekeeping in a boarding house near the steel mill, some form of rape is conceivable, and perhaps even likely. Mary never uttered a word to her progeny about this pregnancy being out-of-wedlock. The baby was born April 19, 1895 and named Antonia.

In late April 1895, Michael Martin Papesh, from Mala Korinj in Slovenia, the lower village, arrived in the United States. On May 6, 1895, less than two weeks later, Michael Papesh, twenty-two, and Mary Perko, twenty-six, were wed at St. Joseph's Parish. Father Sustercic, the founding pastor of the four-year-old parish, presided. Joseph and Theresa Erjavec, whose family remained for decades deeply involved in bringing Slovenians to Joliet to build a new life, witnessed the marriage. The timing of events and the village connections strongly suggest that Mary Perko's and Michael Papesh's marriage was arranged in Slovenia. It seems likely that John and Agatha Meglan Perko from Veliki Korinj negotiated with Michael and Mary Osnik Papesh from Mala Korinj, and then the families sent young Michael to the United States to wed Mary, covering her shame.

Michael and Mary Papesh came together with Antonia, then had five more children: Theresa Rose (1896); Michael Martin, my grandfather (1898); Anton "Doc" (1902); Ann (1904) and Katherine (1909), who died in infancy. On May 30, 1900, Mary Catherine, then eleven, arrived from Slovenia, brought by members of the Erjavec family to join the Papeshes. United with all her children, Mary Perko Papesh settled everyone into one family unit under Michael Martin Papesh's name.

Great-Grandpa Papesh secured a job as a laborer at the American Steel and Wire Company in Joliet when he arrived. By October 2, 1900, the Papeshes were able to purchase a lot for $300 on Ruby Street, a main artery of Joliet. Four doors up from and west of the river, the homestead sat three blocks away from the mill and six from St. Joe's Parish. They spent the next year building their house, constructing it to serve as a residence and a *gostilna*, a boarding house.

While Great-Grandpa labored at the mill, Great-Grandma raised the family and cooked and did laundry for twelve boarders, who worked and slept in alternating twelve-hour shifts. The children helped with chores, which included changing sheets, feeding chickens, weeding the garden in back, helping with the smoke house, and retrieving railroad ties from the river. Great-Grandma used the ties for homestead sidewalk, then sold the rest.

Starting with Aunt Mary, who at thirteen in 1902 had to lie about her age so she could get hired at the match factory, all the children worked as soon as they could to help support the family. The Papeshes raised enough money between November 1909 and May 1919 to buy nine city lots for gardens to raise food for the table. Great-Grandma Papesh traveled by wagon up the Joliet bluffs and then downriver from home to plant, weed, and harvest in the gardens.

In her pictures, Mary Papesh wears dark, shiny dresses. Aunt Gloria told about finding up in the attic, in the 1940s, big aprons that belonged to her as well as the wood cots used for the boarders. In pictures, Great-Grandma's face appears care-worn and serious. The family called her *Doga Mica*, "Big Mary." She ran the house, ran the family, and kept the boarders' money for them, doling it out when they needed it. She was "the Boss." Great-Grandma collapsed from a stroke working in one of her gardens in June 1931. She was sixty-two.

In pictures Great-Grandpa looks stern, his arms folded across his chest. Family rumor had it that he drank. As a little boy, Dad remembered his grandfather breaking up one of the soap-boxes-on-skates Dad kept in the homestead barn. Dad thought his grandfather mean. At sixty-two, Great-Grandpa was hit by a car in mid-December evening twilight and died of multiple skull fractures.

LEADING MICKEY HOME

Great-Grandpa's younger brother, Ignatius James, lived with the family. Uncle Ignac was a laborer all his life, and a janitor at Grandpa's tavern when he died at sixty-four. Unlike his older brother, Uncle Ignac remained a family favorite all his life. All memories of him were fond.

When I planned a trip to Slovenia in 1991, I knew nothing about the name or location of the Papesh home village. I spoke with Dad by phone about what he knew, but he remembered nothing.

The night before I left, Dad called. He remembered an incident when he was four or five years old. Dad was being bounced on Uncle Ignac's knee and laughing. "Hey, Unc, where are you from?" he asked.

Ignac responded in Slovenian, laughing.

Dad said to Grandma, who was also in the room laughing, "What did he say?"

"He said he is from a village named 'big carrots and little carrots,'" his mother reported to little Mickey. "But he is from 'little carrots.'"

The Slovenian word for carrots is *koren*, close to Korinj, the village name. This story was the main clue that led me to the family village near the mouth of the Krka River when I got to Slovenia. Fond memories of Ignac became the clues that led us into our whole family's Old World history.

We have two pictures of Uncle Ignac. In one he is a mustachioed teen wearing the uniform of the Austrian Emperor's army. In the other, taken when he was in his early sixties, he stands talking with a young man at the side door of Grandpa's tavern. His half-smile and wrinkled face look kindly, but wistful, defeated. He died of a heart attack in December 1944. Uncle Ignac left Dad a beautiful engraved gold watch and three sets of gold cuff links, one of woven gold wire, one of gold hexagons angled and hinged, and one of large opals mounted in gold. A proud man, in his youth Ignac clearly was something of a dandy.

The Vesel side of the family – *vesel* means *happy* in Slovenian – arrived in the United States at the turn of the nineteenth to the twentieth century. Leopold Vesel and Ursula Bolte came from villages ten miles apart on a fertile, wooded plain of southeast Slovenia close to the Kamnik Mountains bordering Croatia.

Ursula Bolte's mother, Anna Brezovar, was born December 19, 1842 in the little village of Crmoznjice. At twenty-two in 1865, she bore a child out-of-wedlock. That same year she married Janez Cesar, a man twenty-two years her senior. She bore two children with him before he died in 1869. Anna then moved to the Brezovar farm with her three children. In 1877, she married Franc Bolte. Born February 13, 1849, Great-Great-Grandpa Bolte was over six years Anna's junior. Great-Great-Grandma bore five more children: Ana (1876), Ursula (1878), Ivana (1880), Terezija (1881), Franciska (1883) and Alojzija (1886). The second child of her father and fifth of her mother, my great-grandmother, Ursula Bolte, was born September 15, 1878.

The Vesels came from Smihel, a farm village some ten miles north and west of Crmoznjice. The Petan family, cousins to the Vesels, came from that same village.

Great-Grandpa Vesel arrived in the United States in the late 1890s with his brother Charles and cousin Franc Petan. They, too, worked at the American Steel and Wire Company. On September 1, 1900, Leopold Vesel bought land for a house on Broadway street, one block north and three blocks west of Papeshes, within walking distance of the mill and St. Joe's.

In 1902, after the house was built, Leopold Vesel brought Ursula Bolte over from Slovenia to wed. Family stories have it that the ship sank on the way and Ursula Bolte arrived at the Joliet train station with only the clothes on her back and a note with her name on it pinned to her coat.

Leopold, twenty-seven, and Ursula, twenty-three, were married May 29, 1902. That day the canal flooded. The wedding party and family had to drive wagons from the river bluffs down through flood waters to the old St. Joe's. The bride and groom stood on boards lain across the pews for the ceremony, as did the priest and their witnesses: her sister and his brother. Their wedding picture shows Great-Grandpa Vesel serious but at ease; Great-Grandma Vesel looks tense, almost glum.

The Vesels lived on Broadway Street next door to the Frank and Theresa Petan family. Cousins had married sisters. The Vesels had eight children: Anna (1903); Leopold, called Lee (1905); Edward (1907); Albert William, called Bill (1909); Mary, called Mae (1912); Helen (1914); Raymond (1916) and Leonard (1918). Seven survived into adulthood. Just under two years of age, Raymond was killed when, sitting on the rear porch, his buggy rolled forward down five steps and threw him onto the sidewalk. Raymond died within months of Uncle Leonard's birth.

Grandma Papesh, the eldest Vesel child, remembered her father as a warm, happy man. She would run to meet him when he came home from work, walking up Broadway St. with his lunch bucket in hand, delighted to see her. He grew grapes in the backyard and made wine in the basement. Grandma also remembered him as well-dressed, always in a suit, white shirt, and tie for Sunday Mass. Great-Grandpa died suddenly in his sleep of a heart attack in 1923, at the age of fifty-one. The seven Vesel children then ranged in age from twenty-one down to five.

Dad remembered Great-Grandma Vesel's house as always open, smelling of fresh baked bread eaten with fresh jam out of a wax-topped jar. Dad also remembered going by Vesel's every morning to meet Uncle Leonard, who walked with him to school. While Dad dressed himself at the age of six, his grandma was still putting on her twelve-year-old son Leonard's shoes and socks.

Pictures of Great-Grandma Vesel show her smiling but withdrawing from the camera. Dad said his grandmother remained a recluse most of her life. Gloria, more defensive but still truth-telling, would say, "She never went out because there was no place to go!" Dad's remarks suggested his grandmother never recovered from her life's suffering, especially the ship's sinking on her way to the United States and Raymond's death. Great-Grandma Vesel died of heart failure in 1938 at the age of fifty-nine.

Strangely, the family has pictures of Great-Grandpa and Great-Grandma Vesel lying in their caskets. When I asked Grandma Papesh one time why she would have such a picture, she said she treasured it. It was, after all, the very last time she saw her mother and father.

Grandpa and Grandma Papesh, scions of the Slovenian immigrant struggle, spent their lives broadening and deepening their heritage to make life better for themselves and their children through hard work, first at the store, then later at the tavern. High expectations and work pervaded their lives.

Slovenians, for instance, felt passionate about cleaning. Saturday was cleaning day at the Papeshes. Every Saturday, starting at 8:00 A.M., each room on the main floor of the house was emptied of the furniture that could be easily removed, and the room was then cleaned. The furniture was dusted, then replaced in the room. Grandma taught Dad the routine quite early. He grew efficient about it, usually finishing by noon. Aunt Gloria, on the other hand, hated the work. She would hide in the basement pantry or lock herself in the bathroom and cry. Her mother never let her off the hook. Grandma was known to have waited until nine o'clock at night for Gloria's cleaning to begin.

Saturday afternoon and evening typically meant work at the tavern as well, but it always ended by 8:00 P.M. because Grandma wanted to get home so she could be ready for church in the morning. She took Dad and Gloria home with her.

LEADING MICKEY HOME

Sunday remained relatively free for everyone but Grandpa. Unless Dad served Mass, Grandma, Dad, and Gloria went together to St. Joe's for the eight o'clock Slovenian Mass. Grandma sang in the choir. I remember well into my teens hearing her distinctive alto grinding out hymns in Slovenian. After Mass, Grandma insisted that Dad remain in his suit the whole day. Fastidious about his appearance, something of a dandy – Mom's mother once quipped, "If he's not careful he's going to cut his legs to ribbons with those creases" – Dad always wore good clothes and his shoes always gleamed. Often, he would spend Sunday afternoon at the show, two blocks west up Ruby Street, usually alone. His work at the tavern and the family's Sunday routine kept Dad at arm's length from his peers.

Because the Vesels were close as a family, lived near one another and were dedicated visitors, they often stopped by each other's homes on Sunday afternoons. Ed and Josephine Vesel, Helen and Roy Keith, Lee and Rose Vesel, or Bill and Helen Vesel usually stopped in unannounced. The reverence for one another I saw in those brothers and sisters as a child, which spilled over to all their children, suggested a deep love for each other, dedication to each other in the tough times, and a spirit of fun among them. They loved to laugh and especially talk.

The family kept this pattern during the 1930s and '40s, but it shifted during the 1950s.

Both of his parents favored obedient, polite, trustworthy, responsible, and well-dressed Mickey. His marriage to Mom, however, began an emotional rift between him and Grandma. Because Dad borrowed so heavily from Grandpa, money concerns deepened the rift. Though daily together at the tavern, Grandma experienced Grandpa as emotionally absent from at least 1933. Grandma spent money on clothes to compensate. As she grew distant from Dad after his marriage, Grandma relied emotionally more and more on Gloria, especially after her 1950 marriage when Gloria and John Farkas moved upstairs on Ruby Street. Grandma's emotional redirection and the strength of Gloria's personality meant that Gloria came to dominate Papesh family life.

During 1952, Grandpa went to the money box in the back closet of the tavern to find $150 missing. No one ever formally owned up to anything. Gloria, however, was suspected. She tried to blame Dad, but Grandpa knew that she was the only one who could have taken it. Grandpa told Dad on the side one time that he felt very deeply hurt that Gloria would do such a thing. The money was not the issue, trust was. From that point on, a rift grew between Grandpa and Gloria. I remember overhearing Grandpa talk about the stealing incident even eight and ten years later.

Nineteen fifty-nine through 1960 marked a turning point for the Papeshes. In mid-summer 1959, the tavern cook, Clark Hously, died. Clark's cooking grounded the tavern's appeal. His living in the tavern's back room gave it security. Both were lost. Though I was only eight, I remember being stunned by his death myself. Clark's death meant that the tavern restaurant changed forever. Grandma cooked sometimes, but her meticulous habits left her unable to keep up the demands of a commercial kitchen, so Grandpa was reduced to keeping the kitchen open only on an erratic, part-time basis. Customers gradually dwindled away. Grandpa also began sleeping at the tavern to secure it at night. Meanwhile, Grandma slept alone.

In early 1960, the van lines for which Gloria's husband, John, worked relocated west of the tavern, outside town, bordering the State-ville Penitentiary farms. The company offered John, their manager, the large house on the property that belonged to an unsettled estate. Gloria and John took it.

Gloria, John, Johnny, and Jerry's moving out from the upstairs apartment on Ruby Street created a crisis for Grandma. She refused to stay home alone. Gloria offered to have Grandma and Grandpa both move into their new place since they had four bedrooms on the second floor. They could sell the Ruby Street house then, and have a place, though in the opposite direction, just as close.

Grandpa hated the idea. However, Grandpa and Grandma were sixty-one and fifty-six, had been married for thirty-five years, and were living under enormous stress. Their marriage hovered near the breaking point. He gave in. This motivated Grandpa to settle the twenty-four-year-old will contest and sell Ruby Street in May 1960. Grandma moved in with Gloria and John. Though Gloria says Grandpa stayed in the house for a time, none of us believes that Grandpa ever spent even a single night under her roof. He slept at the tavern. Grandma continued to sleep alone.

In 1969, while Grandpa lived in Clark's old room at the back of the tavern, Grandma still lived with Gloria. Energetic at sixty-six, singing in the parish choir, and involved in parish societies, Grandma still occasionally helped cook at the tavern. Little Jackie Farkas, Gloria and John's youngest child, born in late 1964, went everywhere with her. Grandpa continued to run the tavern. Stooped and thin, his skin hanging loose at his arms and neck, Grandpa hobbled to and from the bar with the aid of a walker. His white socks showed across his shoes' toe box through the leather splits creasing them. He was, as always, available only at the tavern and already host to the cancer that would take his life.

After years of pressure from Dad and Gloria, Grandpa finally sold the tavern that year for $60,000. He and Grandma moved into an apartment on Joliet's west side, near the new St. Joe's Hospital, to begin retirement.

In the spring of 1970, Grandpa was diagnosed with throat cancer. Roger traveled with Grandpa and Grandma to Mayo Clinic for Grandpa's final diagnosis and laryngectomy. Roger remembers vividly Grandpa's trembling lips as Grandma bent down to the gurney to kiss him as they spoke together for the last time.

Grandpa recovered well enough to drive, come to family events, get about town in his walker and communicate through airy grunts, or a note pad and pencil. His humor and natural love of people kept him going. At home in the apartment, Grandma cared for him in her habitually meticulous way, blunt with stories about cleaning his throat tube, putting him on and off the bedpan and even breaking-up his hard stools with her finger. At the end of that year, though, Grandpa's left leg started to ache. The doctors called it sciatica. By early 1971 he quit walking, growing worse. He was hospitalized in the spring of 1971.

I last saw Grandpa Papesh on April 11, 1971 – Easter Sunday. I felt wrenching sadness and anxiety as I saw him lying in a hospital bed in near-screaming pain. Dad later remarked, "Thank God Dad had his larynx out, or they would have heard him screaming through the whole hospital."

Michael Martin Papesh III died of bone cancer May 11, 1971. At his small funeral at St. Joe's, Msgr. Butala, his classmate, still the pastor, presided. A college junior, I took the liberty, before beginning the first reading, to thank everyone for coming. It was the last public ministry of any sort I performed at St. Joe's. Grandpa Papesh's was the first funeral at St. Joe's celebrated in white vestments, and Msgr. Butala seemed none too happy about it. Dad confessed later that burying his father left him understanding the funeral business for the first time.

Grandma Papesh lived another fourteen years. She went back to living with Gloria and her family, spending time putzing around the house and traveling to and from church with her granddaughter, Jackie, and her friend and cousin, Rose Petan Sczepaniak. Even as Alzheimer's and Parkinson's gradually set in over the years, she managed to live happily surrounded by family.

In April 1983, Grandma fell in her bedroom. She likely had had a stroke. She never again spoke. Afterward, Gloria wheeled her through the house, fed her baby food at the kitchen table, and had her sit with the family whenever visitors came; yet Grandma remained mostly bed-ridden. Gloria bathed and cared for her, as did other members of her family, especially Jackie. When Grandma's money ran out, Public Assistance helped.

The last time I saw Grandma Papesh, she was lying on her left side in a fetal position on a hospital bed in her lavender bedroom. It was late evening. A solitary yellow light bulb over her bed lit the room. Pictures of the family hung on the wall nearby. A polka played softly in the background. As I looked down on her, I reflected on her lifelong vigor and strength, now ebbed away, as well as on her many losses. In a brief flash, I wondered if the only way Grandma could cope with so many losses was to stiffen and fall silent. I felt abysmally sad. I was also struck by how much Dad resembled his mother.

Anna Dorothy Ursula Vesel Papesh died March 1, 1985. Though the obituary reads otherwise, I was unable to fly out for Grandma's funeral because a blizzard shut down the St. Paul-Minneapolis airport for the first time in its history.

When Grandma Papesh died, there was little left from the Papeshes to inherit. Jackie Farkas got her car and wore her cameo. Gloria wore Grandma's diamond ring. Our family retained a brass and marble table that belonged to Great-Grandma Papesh, Uncle Ignac's gold watch and cuff links, a cut-glass pitcher and glasses, Grandpa's .38 revolver and Clark's pearl handled one, the keys to the tavern, a pewter lamp from the Papesh's dining room table, and the family pictures. These things serve as our inheritance from Mike and Ann Papesh.

To this day, though, I never smell a cigar, have an Orange Crush, or walk into a tavern without Grandpa Papesh instantly popping into mind. I never eat fried-and-breaded veal, potica or boneless breast of chicken, clean the house or hear a choir sing without immediately thinking of Grandma. And St. Joe's Slovenian Parish served as our family cradle for it all.

•   •   •

After our talk in the rectory, George offered to tour us through the school. Grandpa had left the original school building in fourth grade back in 1908. A new school building was erected next door in 1913. Grandma left that school building in sixth grade back in 1916. Dad and Gloria had graduated from St. Joe's and so had Roger and me. We were delighted with the offer to tour.

Appearing much smaller than I remembered, and far more cluttered, the building smelled the same. As we lingered near plaques commemorating gifts and George told stories about the many donations St. Joe's had received and needed to build-up its enrollment, I found myself wondering if Roger and I were getting a soft-sell alumni tour.

The tour ended at eleven o'clock. We thanked George sincerely and heartily, grateful for his hospitality. "I especially appreciate your willingness to preach, George. It's a tremendous help to me right now."

"Oh, you're welcome, Mike. I am happy to do it. I'll see you tomorrow."

"I'll probably be at the church early to walk around and be nervous – just to warn you. But I'll see you then."

Roger and I both felt happy with the visit and George's kindness. The experience, I mused with Roger, brought us back to our family roots and the values on which our lives rested. George, like us, had been raised at St. Joe's among the Slovenian people. Our families, together, had tilled the Slovenian immigrant soil of a checkered past, romance about America, flight, self-reliance, risk, industriousness, hardship, tragic death, and large family life. Our families, together, got jobs when they came to the U.S. and learned English through the Slovenian community once they settled. The community also kept us profoundly in touch with what the Slovenian people called "the old country."

In St. Joe's church, a flag of the newly independent Republic of

Slovenia graced the side chapel of the Slovenian Madonna, *Maria Po-magaj*. For all of us, the immigrant family experience had been informed, celebrated, offered consolation, and given meaning through the rituals of the Roman Catholic Church and parish life at St. Joe's. George knew, and I knew George knew. Finally, I felt at ease to have George preaching, and let it go.

CHAPTER X
Two Wakes

Roger and I drove back to the motel to pick up Mom and Joe for lunch and the funeral home visit. To my surprise, Joe was in a coat and tie, Mom in a black and white linen suit. They were ready to go.

We sat and talked together about our time with George, then walked across the road to the Louis Joliet Mall to find lunch. Barren of any eatery truly interesting, we finally settled on eating at the food court, each of us finding whatever we wanted. Lunch was a hodgepodge of foods and conversation. The open, spare, cold atmosphere of the food court left me feeling like we were eating in a bathroom, and what I felt seemed to have spread. Our conversation was rather like the room. I was preoccupied by what was to come; I suspected we all were. After lunch, we killed some time ambling through the empty mall until it was time to go.

We arrived at the funeral home at one o'clock. A large, gray building, the place looked like an exaggerated version of the neo-colonial homes found in any upscale suburb at the opening of the twenty-first century. McMansions they were sometimes called. The interior was new hotel lobby, soullessly warm with dainty furniture that left the sitter alert and edgy, as if no one was ever expected to sit back and relax.

Ushered by a receptionist to love seats near a marble, gas fireplace, we waited for Jeff Dames. Two young men wandered back and forth through the open area between us and the door. Mom suspected them to be Freddie and Brian Dames, but it had been so long since she had seen the boys that she felt unsure.

After ten minutes, a young man approached and introduced himself as Jeff Dames. Nearing forty, of average height with dull blonde hair, Jeff wore a blue-gray suit with a royal blue shirt and gray-blue tie that took the edge off a full face, direct blue eyes, and wide chest that suggested the strength and self-possession of a former athlete grown accustomed to giving orders and sitting back while others ran to fulfill them. "Hello, I'm Jeff Dames."

"I'm Michael Papesh, Jeff. I am pleased to meet you. This is my mother and step-father, Mary Jean and Joe Arado, and my brother, Roger."

They met comfortably and Jeff registered no response to Mom and Joe's identity. I recalled the story a funeral director once told me about an advance viewing during which a father beat-up on the body of a son who had committed suicide, demanding to know why he had done it. I felt sure Jeff was prepared for almost anything imaginable from a grieving family.

"I remember you from when you were a little boy, Jeff," Mom said.

Mom radiated warmth enough that Jeff's brother, Freddie, who was walking nearby, came over and introduced himself. Clean-cut, boyishly handsome, with fair skin and dark hair, having none of Jeff's reserved self-possession, Freddie brought ease to our gathering.

Brian came over, too, as he passed by. Thin, narrow-faced, polite, Brian offered his professional hello, leaving his older and younger brothers to engage us. Friendly and gracious, but oddly impersonal, I wondered if they remembered Mom at all really. A quick-arrived lull and Jeff's keeping to business saved us all. "Please come with me," Jeff said with his hands enfolded mid-chest in a preacherly, patronizing sort of way. "I will take you in to see Mike."

Jeff took us around a corner to the right into a dark oak hallway, then opened double doors on the left to a funeral chapel. Dad lay in a casket at the distant wall beyond one hundred empty cream-colored chairs.

"I will leave you for now," Jeff said. "If you have any concerns, I will be available in the office." He closed the doors.

Though we all walked together to the casket, I felt utterly solitary, my attention riveted on the body. Dad wore a black suit and white shirt with a blue and black tie with yellow flecks in it. The clothes seemed to be exactly what he wore in his last formal portrait some three years earlier. Wrapped around his hands was a large gold and oval pearls rosary that had belonged to Grandma Papesh. He wore his glasses. His folded hands displayed all the delicacy of the artist he was as an embalmer. His mouth, however, had been poorly set by the Florida embalmer, so the body's resemblance to Dad was incomplete. I took in the details, feeling nothing.

Mom broke the silence. "Aren't these flowers awful! They're way too much."

On the bottom half of the casket sat a fantastical arrangement of red roses as high as the open lid. It covered the foot of the casket completely. The card said the arrangement was from Lil. "They really are overwhelming, aren't they?" I rejoined.

"Look at this," Roger said. At the head of the casket was a six-foot stand that held a large horseshoe shaped hoop of green leaves measuring some four feet tall and nearly three feet wide. At the top of it, an arrangement of yellow roses with a large yellow bow poked out.

"Who's that from?" Mom asked.

"Tina and Lynn," Rog answered.

Mom moved off from the foot of the casket to read the cards on the other flower arrangements.

"Look, one from Joanie!" she blurted. Mom's sister had sent an arrangement of spider mums and daisies.

"Oh dear! That won't go down very well," I said, suspecting that the best possibility for Lil's response to an arrangement from Mom's sister would be testy confusion. Clearly Joanie sent the arrangement for Roger and me.

"Who are these people?" Mom asked of another arrangement.

I went over to check the card. "I guess this is from some people who work with Lynn."

Joe stood near the casket saying nothing, standing still. Roger stood nearby.

I walked close to the casket to see Dad. Four roses were tucked in the casket with him. "I'm glad about what we did. What do you think?" I asked Rog.

"Yeah, me too, Mike."

"Isn't the casket great?" It was a medium colored oak, but elegant.

"Yeah. I'm glad we did that, too."

"Yes, it's wonderful," Mom chimed in. "He would be happy with that."

"But you sure can't see much of the casket," Roger added. Red roses spilled everywhere, it seemed.

"No, but the casket will be quite stately at the church and cemetery," I said. "That's where it will work best."

Several moments fell vacant. A sense of completeness welled up in me. Dad, Mom, Rog, and I had this last chance to be together. That felt right and good. The three of us standing at Dad's casket brought the four of us together once again as family. We had always been that, I realized, even after the divorce. Now, with Dad gone, I felt no doubt or emotional noise, only warmth and calm. A weight had lifted. I felt grateful that Joe had stepped back silently and let everything be.

"Well," I said with a sigh, "I guess everything is okay for this afternoon."

Everyone took my remark as a signal and silently we turned and left the chapel. When we moved around to the office no one was in the hallway or entry.

"Excuse me for a moment. I want to see Jeff," I said to the family.

I went into the office and asked for Jeff. Mom, Joe, and Rog remained in the foyer. Jeff immediately came around the corner from somewhere.

"Jeff, is there anything we need to touch base about?"

"Yes, Father. I would like for you to see the invoice."

He took out a legal-size sheet that listed the services and costs. "If you would, I have a place for you to sign here and for your brother to sign below."

Roger, always a little nervous about money, felt downright touchy these days about his credit. I preferred that he keep his balance. "Jeff, I will sign but my brother will not. Everything will come through me and you will be paid by the end of the month."

"That will be fine, Father." He handed me a pen and I signed.

"Was everything all right, Father?" he asked blandly.

"Yes, Jeff, everything was fine, except for Dad's mouth. It was poorly set. It didn't look like him. I imagine he arrived that way."

"Yes, Father. I noticed that. I felt around his mouth and his teeth are in. I think they put some material in there to fill him out because he lost so much weight and that distorted the mouth. There's really nothing we can do."

"I expected as much. That's fine. Thank you for everything." I reached out to shake his hand.

"You're welcome, Father."

I left the office to find Mom, Joe, and Rog bantering with Freddie and Brian. The moment I came near, everyone began stepping back to end the conversation. We said our farewells and walked to the car.

"Well, now for the wake," I said as we opened the doors to get in.

"I think everything is going to be just fine, Mike," Mom said. "The Alzheimer's took a lot out of him, but he looks okay."

"And they will like the casket," Roger added. "I am glad we did that."

"Yeah," Mom said. "Everything's going to be fine."

We chatted lightly as we drove back to the motel in rain. I felt calmer since the touchiest and potentially most emotionally explosive part of the funeral was now done, and because of what it had revealed. The wake, I thought, would not be too terribly difficult. I needed some rest, though, so I could make the transition. When we got upstairs in the motel, I told the others I needed to get my clothes off and lie down. Roger said he needed the rest as well. Mom and Joe were fine with it.

It was about one-thirty when I undressed to my shorts and got into bed. Roger did the same.

"Rog, what did you feel when you saw Dad? I didn't feel anything."

"I didn't feel anything either, Mike."

"Really?"

"Nothing at all," he said with a half-distaste and half-indignant expression.

"It amazes me, Roger. The man was my father. I felt nothing. I only just realized that I let him go years back."

"Me, too, Mike. He said he cared but he didn't want to participate in our lives. He was too busy with Lil and partying around Florida trying to forget his pain."

"Wow! Amazing!" I had never put it together quite that way.

"Hey, Mike, look at it this way," he said with a glint of trouble in his eyes. "This is grief at its best!"

We both laughed.

We awoke about a quarter to three to get ready for the wake. I had brought along Uncle Ignac's woven gold cuff links for the occasion as a way of celebrating Ignac's and Dad's relationship, tender care that Dad said he cherished.

Roger donned a gray suit and blue-gray tie. He wore his IBM gum-shoes. His collar was folded up in back, his belly hung over his belt, and the top of the trouser zipper was stressed. I straightened his collar, suggested he do a little work on the bottom of his shirt where it met the trousers and suggested further that he keep his coat buttoned. He was docile about it all. I was grateful that I had told him when I invited him for the dedication that there was one condition: he had to have a haircut within two weeks before coming. Happily, he had done that. He looked just fine and clearly could not have cared less. I appreciated his patience and cooperation with my being a twit about appearances. I was my father's son and Rog seemed at ease with that.

Roger and I bade farewell to Mom and Joe, then chatted lightly in the car on the way down to the funeral home. I felt nervous and suspected Roger felt even more so. We played it easy, knowing each other too well to wonder how the other was feeling, or to stir up one another's emotions when we knew we had to be "on" in just a few minutes. We parked the car and went into the funeral home together. It was 3:40 P.M. I felt no compunction about our being late.

We walked side-by-side into the chapel. Five people stood down front at the casket. Gloria, Jerry, and Jackie stood talking near the foot of the casket. Lil and Lynn stood talking a little distance away from the head of the casket.

Placing herself directly in our path, Gloria walked down to meet us and embraced both of us warmly. She looked as she had for the last eighteen years, wearing a loose many-shades-of-blue, jacket-like top in a leaf pattern with black slacks, stockings, and black leather clogs. The true-red lips, painted eyebrows, false eyelashes, and stiff brown hair worn up, with a slight pouf and short front wave, fit her large frame and ebullient personality like the peel on an apple.

Gloria immediately dove in. We were family. "You should have seen the explosion here a few minutes ago."

I gave her a quizzical look, knowing better than to say anything.

"When Lillian saw those flowers from Joanie Crowther, she hit the roof. 'What business do they have being there! They should be taken away,' she said. I tol' her, 'Hey, Lillian, you're not the only mourner here. The boys are going to be here too. Joan Crowther had a relationship with Mick.'"

155

"He gave her away at her wedding," I happily added.

"Right. So, I told her she had to remember she wasn't the only mourner here. I also said, 'Besides, who knows, maybe Mary Jean will show. You never know.'"

Gloria had "street smarts" beyond what she even knew. If she were a manipulator instead of a straight-shooter, Roger and I would have been in terrible trouble. Happily, what she said could be taken at face value.

"I'm sorry to hear that happened," I responded, hoping to bring the issue to rest. "Oh, well. What can you do?"

Roger added with wry humor only I understood, "Hey, it could be a lot worse."

There was something about the second children in our family that was a little too playful for my relatively anxious and proper disposition, and two second children were beginning their dance. It was time for me to exit. "I want to go over and see Lil," I said. Roger followed.

On the way, we greeted Jerry and Jackie. Huge, wearing a red shirt and black slacks, Jerry's face had the full, flat, happy look of Grandpa Papesh on his wedding day. Calm, light-hearted, without ambition, and having a voice sounding always on the verge of laryngitis, Jerry spent his life as a union carpenter and looked forward to retirement at fifty, in four years, after thirty years of service. During the previous six years he had lived with a woman named Gloria who had a son with disabilities; they never married because Jerry would then have had to assume the financial support the boy now received from the government. The unsightly bulge at the right side of Jerry's stomach he explained as a hernia he would be having repaired later in the summer.

Jackie, single at thirty-six and about to finish her bachelor's degree in nursing, embraced us awkwardly, as always. Never pretty, with close-set eyes and no bridge to her nose, intellectually slow but a hard worker, Jackie was a dear person who shot straight and showed humor in family settings but remained socially withdrawn. Roger and I never really knew her because of our age difference. She always seemed a diamond in the rough, very much like Grandma Papesh, with whom she spent so much time as a child.

We then went over to Lil, who was deeply engaged in conversation with Lynn, and probably felt more nervous than Roger and I put together.

Lil's appearance managed to look overdone even as "the widow." At seventy-five, Lil maintained a petite, hourglass figure, and fresh tan. She wore black spiked heels, black nylons, and a black wrap-around dress with a rhinestone brooch at the bottom of the neckline. The brooch broke the ensemble from the neck down but fit the whole. Her coif was a new shade, the deep brown-red of a maple leaf in late fall, teased high on top and in back, swooped behind her ears, with bangs in front. It looked like a lion's mane, as if fashioned on a Styrofoam bust before being placed on her head. Complementing her too-defined eye makeup, hair-matching lipstick and the bronze tan, her hair gave Lil's square-jawed, worry-worn face a hardness that made it appear glamour-deflated. Dad, of course, had liked all the bunting. It reinforced his sense of prowess. Though I had no reason to expect anything else, I felt disappointed.

"Hello, Lil. My sympathies to you." I embraced her. Roger did likewise.

"Hello, Michael. Thank you. Hello, Roger." Cool grief.

"Hi, Lil. I'm sorry," Rog said as he embraced her.

"Thank you." Cool grief even with Roger. They always connected better than we did. I was surprised.

Lynn stood right next to her with a hesitant, but expectant look on her face. I went to her immediately.

"Hello, Lynn. My sympathies to you."

"Hello, Michael," she said with her Chicago twang. "It's good to see you, and you, too, Rog. Thank you."

I remained surprised that the possibility of Roger's and my grief, or that we might appropriately be extended sympathy, failed to be acknowledged. I let it go.

Lynn, two years older than I, a little taller than her mother and recently trim, was in a casual black dress, nylons, and shoes. Her hair, always bleached blonde, was teased but combed straight down, then flared at the bottom. It looked like a Nazi helmet made of straw.

I turned to Lil. "How are you?"

"Oh, okay," she said with a sigh. "I am glad I took your advice and stayed. I rested the last few days. I didn't get much sleep, but I feel better. It's hard." She would never have stayed had it not been Lynn's advice, too. As for the sleep, she had been an insomniac for the twenty-five years I had known her.

"Yeah, it is," I responded. "But the wake should help."

Roger nodded agreement. Solicitous care was written all over his face.

"Have you seen Dad?" Lil asked.

"Yes, we stopped by earlier today."

"Doesn't he look nice?"

Out of courtesy to Lil, we walked over to the casket to see. For all the artistry Dad applied to embalming and cosmetology himself, I never understood the question Lil asked when people asked it. Nobody I had ever seen, for all the embalmer's effort, looked like the real person, much less nice. In fact, I was surprised at how little a sense of Dad's presence I felt standing at his body.

Gloria came over. "I put these in with him," she said, drawing our attention to two snapshots she had placed at Dad's left arm just below our flowers. "I found this one of him and Lil, and then I put in this one of him and his girlfriend, the last time she was down in Florida."

The second picture was of Dad and Grandma Papesh. I immediately assumed, wickedly, that the picture of Dad and Lil permitted Gloria the indulgence of placing the picture of Dad and Grandma. Gloria pushed the edges, as always, but tried to mind herself as best she could. I thought the snapshots tacky but held no illusions about the status of my opinion. I said nothing, nor did Roger.

There was a bit of commotion behind us.

"Well, you got here!" Gloria said.

The commotion was Gloria's son, John Michael, with four young people, his children whom I had never met. We walked to greet Johnny, moving to where the chairs began from off the foot of the casket.

John Michael, a year younger than Roger and older than Jerry, turned out to be a stocky, large-chested man with a high hairline and dull blonde hair combed straight back into short curls near his neck. John pulsated with the Papesh ego and wound-up-tight Papesh energy Roger and I displayed only when we were anxious. I had had a couple of ulcers and got headaches. Roger smoked, drank gallons of too-sweet coffee, and had headaches. John Michael had had a heart attack at forty-six. Rog and I felt blessed.

Over the years, John had driven semis like his father. Then he sold mortgages. Something of a wheeler-dealer, he now did no-one-was-quite-sure-what. He wore a tee-shirt and white Levi's with tennis shoes. Married at twenty-five, he divorced at thirty-eight, and remarried at forty-one. The children, three boys and a girl ranging in age from fourteen to nineteen, were endowed with their father's gritty discipline, straight talk, strong work ethic, high priority on family, and slightly embarrassed tender care. John Michael was every inch his mother's son.

"Hi, you guys. I thought I would stop in. I gotta go to work in a few minutes but I wanted to see Mike and Rog and Uncle Mick."

We shook hands and John Michael pointed out Johnny, Jim, Joe, and Julie for us. They shook hands with us, and three proceeded to move over to Jackie and Jerry. Johnny, the eldest, held back to talk with John Michael, Gloria, Rog and me. Looking least like his father, Johnny was self-possessed, comfortable, talkative, and matter-of-fact. His ambition was to become a car mechanic and it had dawned on him, he said, that he needed to go to junior college for a couple of years to prepare for that. John was supportive, but said Johnny had to pay for school, too. They understood each other perfectly, but Johnny clearly liked pushing the edges with his dad. John Michael needed challenge to feel fully alive and his good-natured eldest son seemed the ideal candidate to offer it.

As the conversation wound down, the time approached four o'clock. A couple of people appeared at the chapel door. After a brief visual survey, I decided that where we happened to be standing, if unusual, was probably best for the reception line. The register stood at the main chapel door on the other end of the room from us. The Mass card stand sat down the wall, perpendicular to and near the foot of the casket. I stood there with Roger next to me. Jerry and Jackie stood on the other side of Roger towards the casket. Gloria stood at the foot of the casket. Lil stood front and center. This positioning left me the first person to take everyone's hand and greet them with, "Hello, I'm Michael Papesh." I would then introduce people to Roger. The two of us could then huddle or split, depending on who came and the length of the line.

While I appreciated that Jerry and Jackie had a strong enough family sense to assume a place in the reception line, I thought it odd that they took that place at all. As the evening proceeded, they stepped back and let folks move to Gloria. The line ended at Gloria and Lil. They spoke with people at Dad's body, occasionally together, most often apart. Lynn took a seat.

The arrangement seemed sensible. Roger and I held the position of hospitality, seeing everyone and helping them feel at home, while affording those who wanted to see us specifically ample room and time to do that without offending or interfering with Lil. Gloria was comfortably in between, doing as she wished. The line seemed something of a symbol of reality for each of us and all of us together, certainly for Roger and me.

The very first visitor was George Reid and his wife. Near sixty, George had been an apprentice embalmer at Dames Funeral Home in the early 1970s and remained in touch with Dad the rest of his life. Dad always took special interest in the apprentices. Dad's very practical sense of the funeral business brought home to them the nitty-gritty particulars of funeral directing day-to-day and the secrets to superlative embalming. Gregarious, hungry to learn, and a quick study, George was foremost among the apprentices for Dad. Though we only had a chance to speak briefly in the line, George stayed behind for an hour or so sitting in the chapel with his wife. On my way from a brief bathroom break later in the wake, I stopped over to see him.

"Thanks for coming, George. Dad had very special affection for you throughout the years."

"He was a great man to me, Mike."

"I need to mention something to you. I was talking with Jeff and he mentioned that the Dames' appreciated Dad very much, so much that he was the only one they were willing to leave alone in the building." George's eyebrows raised. "I thought things were different from that, George."

"Boy, were they! Your dad held the place together, Mike. He was the reason guys like me stayed. You can ask any of the guys who worked there. The Dames boys didn't know what was going on."

•　　•　　•

When Dad started at Fred C. Dames Funeral Home on January 1, 1965, a man on staff named Cecil Thayer drove for funerals, helped make arrangements with families, hovered at wakes, and did various managerial tasks, including keeping equipment and sundries in stock. Cecil was in his sixties. A year or so after Dad arrived, "the brothers," as Dad styled them, which referred to Joel and Mark Dames, called Cecil in and let him go. Both Roger and I registered alarm at the incident. The suddenness of the decision, the brothers' lack of loyalty to their employees that it suggested, the evident dispensability of people on the funeral home staff and, therefore, the relative insecurity of Dad's position it portended, scared us at the time. Though Rog and I were only teenagers Cecil's demise became a cautionary tale for us, a symbol of risk and failure. "Dad, don't let yourself become another Cecil Thayer," we reminded Dad throughout his tenure at Dames Funeral Home.

Though he had a small percentage of the business, Dad became increasingly aware that he was doing the large share of the work and getting too little for it. The runaway inflation of the 1970s complicated life even more. The brothers usually met Dad's requests for salary increases with procrastinating silence. So, Dad tried various methods for getting their attention. He would leave promptly when his hours were up rather than go the extra mile. He bought a new Cadillac in silver with a black vinyl top, unusable for the Dames fleet of dark green Cadillacs. Eventually Mark and Joel would come around, but with a relatively small increase. As inflation galloped, Dad's wages bought less and less.

In 1978, Dad pushed farther still in his attempt to get an increase. He threatened to quit if he failed to get one by a specific date. The date came and went with the Dames' usual silence. Disillusioned, angry, thrashing about emotionally, Dad began to plan a move to Florida. The Dames' let the issue sit for months. By the time Mark approached him with an offer, Dad's plans to move were set in stone. Dad refused, though, to allow disaffection to grow between him and Mark Dames.

Dad and Lil moved to Venice, Florida. Mark and Sharon Dames had a condominium there. Dad, Lil, Mark, and Sharon became eating and drinking friends in Florida, Dad sometimes picking them up at the airport when they arrived. Calling Mark "Junie," short for "Junior" because he was so very much like his father, Dad usually had a story or two about "tying one on" with Mark and Sharon when they had stayed in their Florida condominium. He would share with us from time to time that Mark offered him a position at the funeral home back in Joliet, especially after Joel Dames left the business, but Dad refused it.

Whether from vanity, stupidity or mere miscalculation, Dad had overplayed his hand with the Dames boys, who were sloppy managers holding no loyalties except to themselves. Though she was divorced from Dad at the time he left Dames, Mom felt indignant at them and mystified that Dad continued a friendship with Mark. For our part, Roger and I thought Dad had let himself become another Cecil Thayer.

•　　•　　•

After talking with George, I went back into the reception line, which remained short but continuous for the next hour or so.

Representatives from three staunch St. Joe's families came, pillars of the parish whom I suspected showed up for most everything parish related. A woman and her sister from one family were granddaughters of the couple who sponsored the Papeshes when they came from Slovenia. The husband in another couple had been a grade school classmate of Dad and Lil's, and father of a father and son who came together. All three families had children who had been classmates of mine. All three, too, were loyal to Tezak's, the other Slovenian funeral home. Always courteous to them, Dad nonetheless kept his distance. I instinctively learned to do the same.

Fellow workers of Lynn's, bowling partners of Lil's from years ago, and members of Lil's large extended family also came, notably her mother's sisters. Yvonne Wunderlich, widow of Dad's best friend, Ernie, came with Bill, Ernie's supposed brother. Dad and Mom had long assumed Bill was, in fact, the gift of a seventeen-year-old Ernie's indiscretion. Muggs Videtich stopped by with her son, who was also Dad and Mom's godson, Paul. Old friends of Mom and Dad's since the first years they were married, Muggs and Tony became alienated at the time of Mom and Dad's divorce because they "played both sides" as Mom and Dad each saw it. Muggs proudly showed me a picture of her daughter, the nun. Peggy and I had dated once. Paul looked the spitting image of his deceased father. I had not seen him since he was two. Jane Short, now Hickock, came, a childhood friend whom I enjoyed seeing. Curiosity and happy memories brought her. Mom's cousins, Frederick "Otts" Stoiber, and his wife, Rose, as well as Otts' sister Barbara "Bobbie" Burrill also came. They spoke with Roger and me, but refrained from greeting Lil, understandably enough. Some one-hundred-twenty-five guest names filled the register. Slowly and steadily they came.

While I was greeting the Slovenian community guests, I noticed Dad's cousin, Delores Plut, in line with her husband Alex. I had gotten to know her through her son David, who attended Mass in the late 1980s at the downtown Minneapolis parish where I helped on weekends. I had the privilege of presiding at David and Cheryl's wedding, from the historical perspective a healing event in the Papesh family. Behind Delores and Alex stood a woman I had never seen.

"This is Marge Raker," Delores said, nodding toward her. I instantly noted that Marge was the cousin Gloria had warned me about

"Hello, Marge, I am pleased to meet you." I extended my hand. She wore a white skirt and blouse with a telling red jacket. Petite, salt and pepper hair in a page boy, about eighty, she looked vaguely like the pictures of Aunt Tonka I had seen. She took my hand briefly. Her glance was unflinching.

"Why did you write all that about my mother and my grandparents? Why did you hurt me?" From the family stories I recalled, Marge was very much Tonka's daughter.

"Marge, I am sorry if I hurt you. I had no intention of hurting you at all."

"Why did you write those things?"

"Marge, I searched through documents and put marriage license information together with birth certificate information. It was an accident that I found that out."

"Why are you going through all those things. You shouldn't be going through all those things!"

"Marge, I am just doing genealogy work."

"You shouldn't be going through all those things. My mother died without ever telling me any of that."

Marge evidently felt hurt and ashamed, and that I had violated her and her family. Frankly, I realized later, Tonka may not have known herself the history I had discovered. The Irish family never knew precise facts surrounding some of their births and marriages either. They just avoided celebrating birthdays and anniversaries.

"Marge, please accept my apology. I had no intention of hurting you. Besides, what I found was typical of European families. It's true of my Irish family as well. I don't see it as so terribly serious. It was an ordinary thing to happen, and it's all through both my families."

My sincerity seemed to give her pause. My clerical collar likely helped. "Well," she said after a brief moment. "You still hurt me."

"I am sorry, Marge. Please accept my apology. That was not my intention." Slovenians, like many eastern Europeans, take things personally always, which is one of the messier traits we have had to struggle with as a family.

Since we seemed finished, I introduced her to Roger, and the line began to move again. Rog charmed her briefly and Marge passed on. I now understood much better that Sunday morning argument sixty-five years before that ended in screaming and shouting, with brothers and sisters never speaking again.

Two tall men came through the line, one of whom I recognized instantly as Ross Ferguson. Wally Ferguson, Ross' father, had been a grade school classmate of Dad's and Lil's. Wally and his wife, Lil, came to our Cowles Ave. house with the kids one time. Other than that, I saw Ross only at school. He had been in the class between Roger and me in grade school. Tall and well-built then, Ross was now barrel-chested and silver-gray. He had kept his 1970s middle-of-the-head part. I had not seen him for thirty-seven years, when he was a seventh grader. Pink-faced and youthful looking, he had changed little. I assumed he had come to honor his father's friendship with Dad. I immediately shook his hand. "Hello, Ross. Michael Papesh. This is Roger."

The man with Ross was nearly half-a-head taller than Roger and me. About forty, he was well-built and had a craggy, Mt. Rushmore face. He looked strikingly like his mother. "And is this Billy?" I asked.

"Yes, it is!" he said with a bright smile. "How do you remember?" Clearly a gregarious man with a glint of trouble in his eyes, I instantly liked him.

"Billy went rivers!" I retorted. He blushed. Ross and Roger laughed. "I remember when you were about two or so. You visited our house with your family, and you wet your pants. Your mother said you 'went rivers.' I had never heard that before. It was a wonderful expression!"

"Well, those days are over! It's good to see you guys." Billy had a wide, straight smile that lit the room.

"Thanks, Billy, I am glad to see you, too. It has been a long time."

"Yeah, glad to see you," Rog chimed in.

"I came because your dad had an impact on my life," Billy said. "I was an embalmer for eighteen years, you know!"

I was taken aback. "Really?"

"Oh, yeah. When I was little your dad would drive by and my dad would say, 'There goes Mickey Papesh. Look how clean he keeps those cars!'"

"He certainly did do that," Rog said.

"Well, I saw that and decided that I wanted to become a funeral director, too."

"Wow!" I responded, transported by the story. "Do you work for a funeral home, Billy, or have your own?"

"No. I embalmed for funeral homes around Chicago and Joliet though. It got to be too much for me, so now I have a job at the prison with Ross here." Ross, it turned out, was a pipe fitter at the Illinois State Penitentiary out on Route 53, what we all called Stateville.

"Dad had to do the same thing, Billy," I told him. "For years he embalmed for thirteen other firms in the area. When he was thirty-nine, he had heart problems, so he had to start taking it easy. Luckily, right at that time the Dames boys approached him. Otherwise the work might have killed him."

The line was finished for a time so Billy, Roger and I talked for a long time about family, religion and whatever else came to mind. Ross talked with the Farkases some, but mostly stood near us silently, with his hands folded on his chest. He precisely took the posture I remembered his father taking when I would see him around St. Joe's.

After several minutes, four young women came through the line. They introduced themselves as Bill Kobe's daughters, Lil's nieces. Bill was Lillian's brother. "We're sorry for your loss," one of them said.

I thanked them. Their whole demeanor, however, suggested a line at McDonald's. They evidently felt obliged to greet us, but clearly wanted to get it over with. After they passed through the line, they sat in the front row near Lynn talking together with their family.

Bill and Char, Lil's brother and sister-in-law, came into the funeral chapel at one point, but kept their distance from Roger and me. Bill left after six-thirty or so, then returned with Lillian's Mother, Ann. Toward the end of the evening I went over and sat behind them since there was no room in their row. I greeted Bill and Char. They had nothing to say. Bill just gave me a blank look, hardly mustering the obligatory handshake.

Halfway through the wake time Roger and I took a break together. I needed the restroom and he needed a cigarette. We went outside and talked about the turnout, how people had changed and the coolness of Lil's family toward us.

On our way back in we met Gloria in the foyer, who was herself taking a break. We had not spoken for three hours or so. She was chipper, pleased with the crowd who came.

Jim and Mary Clare Sczepaniak came into the foyer shortly afterward, and the five of us talked briefly. Jim was Dad's second cousin, about fifteen years younger. He and Mary Clare had visited Dad in Florida. I never remembered doing anything socially with them as a child, or hearing of Mom and Dad doing so, but they had visited Dad at the nursing home, they said.

After they walked on Gloria told us that Jim and Mary Clare had taken a picture of Dad during their visit and Lil got angry. "What business do they have taking his picture?" she complained.

Gloria assumed she was upset about the possibility that Dad might not have looked good that day. "What's she bothered by that for? He always looked fine. Besides, they're family!"

I agreed with Gloria but let the remark pass. Neither of us had joined Lil's fan club and I thought it best to avoid igniting a fuse.

The last visitor was Tommy Gasperich. Tommy told us he had played the trumpet near Dad's sax in the Joliet Catholic High School Band until, in his junior year, Dad quit the band to dance with Mom at the socials. Tommy had also been in the wedding party for Mom and Dad's marriage in 1946. He said he liked Dad very much and wanted to pay his respects. Afterward, Roger and I both thought it odd we had never met him before.

By eight o'clock, only the family remained. When we decided for sure the evening had come to an end, Roger and I started to get up to leave when Gloria asked me if I would say a prayer. "Ann Kobe is here, and she won't be able to be at the Mass tomorrow. Say a prayer, Michael. She's very religious and would appreciate it."

I thought it very strange for Gloria to be taking care of Lil's mother and making a bit of a scene about doing so. Knowing well, though, that grief does strange things, I went ahead. Bill, Char and Ann Kobe, Gloria and Jackie, Lillian, Lynn, Roger, and I all joined in an Our Father, Hail Mary, Glory Be and an Eternal Rest Grant unto Him, O Lord. These were the classic Catholic prayers for a funeral. I was glad we prayed, even though I felt confused by Gloria's behavior.

When the prayer was over, Gloria invited Lillian, Roger, and I over to her place for something to eat. We all said we would come. Rog and I had not eaten since lunch.

Since I planned to go to the church instead of the funeral home in the morning, I wanted some time alone with Roger and Dad, whatever would come of it. I had briefed Roger and gave him the high sign. We excused ourselves to remain behind. We told them we would meet them at Gloria's.

When they left, Roger and I knelt at the casket. "It was a strange experience tonight, wasn't it?" I remarked.

"Yeah, but a lot of people came. Yvonne Wunderlich! It was wonderful to see her. She hasn't changed much at all."

"Did you notice, Rog, what they said and didn't say about Dad?"

"They really didn't say much, did they?"

"No. But I think I learned things about him I never knew. Several said what a nice guy he was. One called him very social. I gather the Dad we knew at home was not the Mickey Papesh people knew at the funeral home."

"Yeah, it's like he saved all his energy for being nice to people at the funeral home and then was a son-of-a-bitch at home," Rog rejoined.

"It sure seemed that way. It was as if all his friendships and relationships happened at the funeral home. We really didn't see much of the best side of him, did we?"

"I guess not."

"He was a funny duck, wasn't he?"

"That's our dad!" Rog responded with seeming acceptance, yet quizzical good humor.

"I thought you were wonderful tonight," I said to him.

"It was okay." Roger always felt a little embarrassed when he got a compliment, as if he didn't deserve it. In fact, he had been spectacularly charming all night long.

"Well, I suppose we ought to go," I said, taking off the heat.

"Yep. Food's waiting for us!"

I looked at Dad's body one last time. "It doesn't really seem to be him, does it?"

"No, Mike. It doesn't."

We walked out together silently.

Gloria lived a five-minute straight line drive from the funeral home. We arrived at the same time as Lil and Lynn did. The two of them, with Gloria and Jackie, Roger, and I, sat around the kitchen table as we waited for a lasagna to warm. I made a Slovenian salad, vinegar and oil mixed with iceberg lettuce, and let it sit. We talked lightly about the evening, the food, cats, and dogs. We all had pets. Roger and I stayed about an hour-and-a-half. The conversation helped us all deflate. It felt comfortable. Gloria and Roger kept the talk bouncing along.

Back at the motel, Mom and Joe were up when we arrived. Mom, of course, was curious. We filled them in. Seven or eight people had asked for her. Mom seemed especially tickled by that.

"I grew up with all those people, Mike. I know them lots better than Lil ever did. She was never around."

I felt tired. Rog did, too. After making plans for breakfast, we excused ourselves and were in bed by eleven o'clock. Other than being clear about the program in the morning, Rog and I simply stayed quiet.

CHAPTER XI
The Funeral

I rose before dawn to walk. Even after the events of the past days, it still felt surreal that we were burying Dad. Refreshing and clearing my mind, the walk let God into all I had experienced, and God was good company. When I arrived back at the motel room Roger was up. We spoke about the surreal sense of the day and continued the talk through breakfast. I felt calm, open to whatever would come. Rog seemed so, too.

The one matter I wanted to settle at breakfast was how to handle Roger's transportation during the funeral. I told him I had no plans to go to the funeral home and wondered if he might ride with Lil to the church. Rog thought that would be fine. I suggested we ride together after the funeral Mass and stick together after that. He agreed and preferred handling it that way.

After breakfast we said goodbye to Mom and Joe, then changed for the funeral. I had worn Uncle Ignac's woven gold cuff links for the wake. For the funeral, I decided to wear a sterling silver pair of Bill Bozich's that Lil had given me some years before. I had a mission to accomplish with them.

Roger wore the same outfit as the night before. I helped him straighten a bit, and then took up the vestments I had brought. Several months earlier I had purchased a white chasuble and stole with rose damask and pewter trim for Eastertide wear and for my own funeral. I could think of no better occasion than this one for the vestment to make its debut in front of the family.

I hung the vestments in the car, and we left for the funeral home. At a quarter to nine, I dropped Roger off then drove to St. Joe's. I wanted to be quiet and grounded for what was to come. I had never presided at St. Joe's and thought it might be emotional for me. I wanted to be prepared. Roger understood and I assumed that the family would as well.

•   •   •

Grandma Papesh died on Friday March 1, 1985. Dad called me that day to tell me and presumed that I would come to Illinois for the funeral. So did I. Roger, in California, was not expected. I was.

I arranged a flight for Sunday after Masses so I might attend the Sunday evening wake and preside and preach the Monday funeral. This was to be the first time that I would function as a priest at St. Joe's. I had ambivalent feelings.

When I was to be ordained in 1983, Dad was in Florida, Mom was in Colorado, and Roger in California. While it was customary after ordination to celebrate a Mass of Thanksgiving in one's home parish, none of my immediate family lived in Illinois. Moreover, though old Msgr. Butala was alive, I had never met the current pastor. When I briefly raised the subject with Mom and Dad, they each expressed a lack of enthusiasm about my having a Mass of Thanksgiving there. They each felt awkward about being together and with their spouses for the first time since their divorce and remarriage. They felt less than excited, too, about the travel to Illinois after having traveled to Minnesota for the ordination. I made no overtures to St. Joe's.

At ordination time I received two gifts from the St. Joseph's community. Msgr. Butala sent a check for $300, the largest gift I received, but for Mom's and Dad's. The Altar and Rosary Society, to which my then-homebound grandmother had belonged for decades, and who would ordinarily have put on the reception at St. Joe's Hall, sent me $25. All in all, I felt content not to preside at St. Joe's, though I assumed the day would come.

The night before I was to fly out for Grandma's funeral, a blizzard hit the Twin Cities, shutting down Twin Cities International Airport for the first time ever. I called Dad, who was staying at Gloria's, to let him know that I was stranded in Minneapolis.

"What am I going to do?" he asked.

I thought that a very odd response. "Gee, Dad," I responded, "I am sure the pastor or Msgr. Butala would be happy to preside."

He then gave me his usual response to most everything. "Well, okay, Son."

"Sorry about that, Dad. Please accept my sympathy and give my sympathy to Gloria, too." I let the whole matter go, except to call the family after the funeral to check in.

Some years later, Gloria sent me an extra copy she had found of Grandma's obituary. It read that the funeral Mass was to be a concelebrated Mass with the Reverend Michael. L. Papesh as celebrant. I finally understood Dad's odd response. My having to stay in Minnesota contradicted the death notice, trampling his bragging rights.

•　　•　　•

When I got to St. Joe's before the funeral, the church was open and I headed straight for the sacristy, where I hung up the vestments. I then went out into the church to walk and pray. Every pew, every hat hook, every molding, every picture, statue, and station I recognized as an old friend and felt delighted to see. I remembered the hundreds of daily Masses during our school years. I remembered the high holy days when the statue of the dead Christ was revealed beneath the *Marija Pomagaj* (Mary, help us!) altar at the end of Good Friday, the statue of the Risen Christ carried through the church at the Easter Vigil, and the bells, flower petals, and chains chinkling against censors that greeted the Blessed Sacrament in the Forty Hours processions. I walked, gawked, and reveled in this place that had cradled my faith.

About nine-thirty, a white-haired man and woman came into the church. I paid little attention at first, then recognized them. It was Ella Ryan and her son Larry, Jr. The Ryans had lived one house down and across the street from us on Cowles Ave. between 1958 and 1970. We picnicked and partied with them. Larry Sr., who had died six months earlier at eighty-nine, had been a gadabout in the neighborhood, always stopping in at odd times, getting folks together, and traveling one hundred miles for a brick of bleu cheese or fresh cod. Ella, reserved, dignified, and understated, stood as Larry Sr.'s mirror opposite. She joined in when she had to it seemed. Young Larry, four years my senior, had been part of my inspiration to seminary and my whole inspiration to Quigley North in Chicago as the high school seminary I wanted to attend.

I greeted them and we talked. Larry, though married thirty years and father of four, seemed very much the same, his father's son. Ella, though much older, was the same, too, even after thirty years. I felt moved they had come.

I excused myself from Ryans to get into the sacristy. As I did so, Jane Short Hickok came in. I walked over and greeted her. She said she had come to see me say Mass. I thanked her, then pointed out Larry and Ella in case she might want to join them. She stayed by herself. The Shorts, though part of the neighborhood, moved in five years after we did. They likely traveled in a slightly different orbit. I had followed young Larry to seminary. I enjoyed Ella's tender reserve. Jane may not have known them very well.

When I reached the sacristy, a girl about thirteen was dressed to serve. She seemed disoriented. Though I expected the worst, I explained what I expected. She said she understood. George came in. I asked him what he expected, and he replied that it ought to go according to the book. We were set and ready.

Shortly after the bells began to toll, we walked down the center aisle and met Dad's casket and the family. Lil, wearing under her coat a cranberry and rose paisley top with a black skirt, looked drawn. Gloria and Roger looked sober.

"In the waters of baptism, Michael Leopold Albert Papesh died with Christ and rose with him to new life," I began as I sprinkled holy water on Dad's casket. "May he now share with him eternal life."

As Mass proceeded, I felt surprise that I was no more moved by Dad's funeral than I would have been at the funeral of any parishioner. Indeed, I felt less moved than I had been at many. George's homily was nondescript. He referred to Dad very little. The family seemed quiet and sad. The thirty-five others in the assembly participated minimally. The music was dull, lifeless. The gift of the liturgy was the richness of the Roman Rite itself, and that we were all gathered at St. Joe's. Nothing else mattered.

After the Prayer after Communion, I addressed the assembly on my own and the family's behalf. Though I felt able to say little, I decided that I had to say something. I had settled that in my morning walk.

> On behalf of Lillian, my brother, Roger, my Aunt Gloria, and our whole family, I want to thank you for joining us this morning for the Rite of the Christian Funeral.
>
> Dad's great passion in life was the funeral business. He gave half a century of his life to the corporal work of mercy that is burying the dead. Embalming was an art for him. His service was caring and compassionate. He watched that every detail was done with dignity. There

is no greater tribute we could give Dad than to do well what Dad did so very well.indeed.

In the days ahead, I would ask you to please pray for Lillian, who, for all the difficulty she has known in these more recent years, has lost the center of her life. Please pray for Gloria, who has now lost the whole of her family of origin, the only people who could truly understand much of what she experienced in her early life, especially at the tavern.

As for Roger and me, we will be okay. But please remember us in prayer as well.

With that, I went to the casket and began the Final Commendation.

The Final Commendation was the emotional high point of the liturgy, with the body honored by incense and the commendation prayer. Performing this slow, deliberate act as we prayed that the angels take Dad into Paradise, I felt mildly moved. After the prayer, I proceeded past the casket down the aisle. As I passed it, I kissed the casket about where Dad's head would be. The family burst into tears.

The tenderest I felt during the rite was watching Dad's casket come down the aisle with Roger, Gloria, and Lil following it back to the front doors, all red-faced and in tears. My eyes watered slightly, but I remained composed.

As the casket passed Jeff Dames stopped it. George indicated that I was expected to bless the casket again with holy water, which I did. Then the family passed out to the hearse and their cars.

I went to the sacristy and divested. I thanked George for everything. He apologized he could not go to the cemetery; he had another funeral. I went to the car in front of the rectory. Roger was waiting for me, still flushed, finishing a cigarette.

The car was parked right behind the hearse where Jeff Dames had coached me to park it. The rest of the cortege was on the side of the church. Rog and I got in. I started the engine, then waited.

"Rog, what are the tears about? We have spent so much of this time talking that we felt so little."

"Well, Mike, everyone was crying so I cried."

"Really? That's it?"

"Yeah, Mike. That's it. The end was really emotional, and when you asked everyone to pray for Gloria, she was holding my hand and about broke my fingers."

I gave him a moment or two of silence to regroup. The hearse started to move. We followed. "What happened at the funeral home?" I asked.

"When I got there everyone was sitting down so I took my seat. Gloria said Billy Vesel was there. By the time I greeted the family, though, I didn't have a chance to talk to him because it was time to close the casket." Billy was Dad's first cousin, six years older than Roger and me, and the son of Dad's Uncle Bill, whose real name was Albert. Dad took his confirmation name after Uncle Bill. Billy was the last of his family. Bill died in the 1950s. Helen remarried but was killed in a car crash in the 1970s. Carolyn, Billy's younger sister, died of cancer in her thirties.

"What happened at the closing of the casket?" I was curious. It can be a deeply emotional time and contentious, too. We were now across the bridge, heading up the bluff and passing by the home on Ruby Street where Grandpa had been born and the family had been raised.

"Lil, Gloria, and I stood there. Jeff Dames went systematically through everything, 'What to do want to do with this? What do you want to do with that?' When he asked about the casket cross, Lil said

179

that you would get that. She has it. I am supposed to get the folded flag. The roses and pictures stayed in the casket with him."

"What happened to the rosary?" I asked. I thought the oval shaped pearls rosary a gorgeous thing I had never seen before.

"Gloria said, 'That was Mom's. Let him keep it.'"

"So, it's going to be buried with him?"

"Yeah."

I felt a mild sense of loss at that. "Was Lil all emotional?"

"Yeah. She kissed him on the head and said a couple of things. Gloria touched his hands and said goodbye. I didn't do anything but watch as the casket was closed."

"Who did you ride over with?"

"Lil. Oh! She said that it was nice that we bought the casket. 'It's just as he would have wanted,' she said."

"Really! After all that!"

"Yeah," he said with a smirk.

"It was the right thing to do. It was beautiful."

"Yeah. It was the right thing."

"How are you doing, Rog?" Pain, especially other peoples', was not Roger's long suit. I felt concerned.

"I'm okay."

We had now reached the cemetery. A canopy stood over where the open grave was and a row of chairs sat next to it, outside it. I took the ritual book and we both got out of the car and walked toward the back of the hearse. I took Jeff aside and gave him the precise instructions for the lowering signal. He understood. I then waited with Rog at the hearse door.

Jeff had told me the day before that there were no funeral directors left from Dad's age group, so he had trouble finding funeral director pall bearers, which was local custom. Frankly, I was glad. I wanted to carry Dad's casket.

Jeff, Freddie Dames, John Farkas, Rog, and I took the handlebars on the casket and carried it to the bier. The casket was suspended over the vault and the lid was suspended parallel to it on the opposite side of the casket from the family. The vault covering and lowering were mechanically set up to be a very smooth operation. Everyone took their places. Lil sat in the front row on the far end away from me at the casket's foot.

When we assembled, I began the prayers. At the agreed upon signal, the casket started to lower into the vault, the vault lowered into the ground and the lid lowered over the vault. "Ashes to ashes, dust to dust," I began.

The crowd gasped as the casket began to lower. Lil looked stunned, as if she could not believe what she was seeing, as if she had no idea what to do. Just as the lid was coming to its rest Lil cried out, "Wait!" She seemed to fall back toward her brother Billy behind her.

I felt a surge within, the imperious indignation of satisfied revenge on Lil for all she had done in moving ahead on funeral planning without Rog and me, or even Gloria. The intensity of my feelings instantly told me, from long experience, that they were hooked to ancient, crusty feelings of having been emotionally abandoned as a child, particularly by Dad. I immediately felt ashamed. I hated the feelings. Besides, I wanted the casket lowering in the rite for far nobler reasons.

Lil caught herself, then reached for a rose on her arrangement nearby and placed the rose under the lid, in the vault with the casket. The vault lid lowered into place and the vault continued down into the grave. When all rested on the bottom, the cemetery staff removed the lowering harnesses and the lowering equipment around the grave. The only thing left was the vault down in the open grave.

We prayed intercessions for Dad and the Lord's Prayer, and then asked that eternal rest be granted unto him, perpetual light shine upon him and that he rest in peace. I concluded the prayers with the blessing. "Now, let us go in the peace of Christ."

I stepped back and turned to take a rose from one of the arrangements nearby. I selected a rose from Joanie's rather than from Lynn's or Lil's arrangements. Others in the crowd followed suit. The family and guests slowly milled out toward their cars.

When I got near Roger, I pointed out Larry and Ella Ryan. We went over to them and talked briefly. I asked them to the luncheon, but they said they had to go. Jane Short Hickok was standing alone, so I went over to her and thanked her for coming. She said she had enjoyed seeing me after these thirty years and more and she promised to come by the rectory in Minnesota when she came up.

I noticed Marge Raker out of the side of my eye in a red coat and black velvet collar. I went to her, "Thank you for coming, Marge."

"Take this," she said handing me a $20 bill. "Use it for Masses for your father and my grandparents." She stepped away shyly.

"Thank you, Marge, I would be happy to," I said to her. "Again, thank you for coming." I received her request as a gesture of peace. At the same time, I still heard echoes of the family alienation set firmly that Sunday morning in 1936. I felt mystified at Marge's seeming failure to grasp that Michael Martin and Mary Perko Papesh were my family, too.

Roger was saying goodbye to Ryans when I finished with Marge. Everyone else had gone to their cars.

"Let's go over to the grave and say goodbye, Rog." We went over and stood by the grave, looking in. I put my arm around Rog.

"Well, Rog, there he lies."

"Yeah, Mike, and we did it right."

"He would have liked it."

"I think so, too."

We went over to the car. Jeff Dames was there.

"Thank you, Jeff. Your work was excellent, even through the mess of it all."

"You're welcome, Father. We were happy to be of service."

Rog and I shook hands with him. Rog asked him to remember us to his parents. We got in the car and drove to Al's Steak House on Joliet's south side for the luncheon.

When Rog and I got to Al's we were directed to a private room. The space was set up for about thirty-two, four tables of eight. The St. Joe's folks took one table, which included the Churnovics and Muggs Videtich, old friends of Dad's. Since they were by no means close to us as I experienced the family, I felt surprised they would come to the lunch. The table nearest the door was Gloria's family. The table next to it was Lil's family. The table behind was taken by some extended members of Lil's family. Rog and I were last to arrive.

As Gloria headed toward her family, I took her by the hand. "Let's sit with Lil's family."

She gave me a look that said, 'What the hell are you talking about!'

"Come on," I said. "Just this one last time."

"Okay-ay!" she said. She moved with Rog and me to the table with Lil's family.

I sat next to Lynn, who still wore her fringed helmet. Gloria sat to my right and Roger next to her. Lil sat at Lynn's left, her sister-in-law Charlene next, then her brother Billy across from me. The seat between Billy and Roger sat open. Gloria asked me to say grace, checking it out with Lil, even though some had begun to eat their salads at another table. I stood, invited all to grace, led it, then sat down again.

"The funeral was very nice, Michael. You did a nice job," Lynn began.

I thanked her, then remembered my mission. I huddled with her. "Lynn, see these cufflinks. They belonged to your dad. Your mother gave them to me some years ago. I wore them so I could give them to you today."

"Keep 'em," she said without a blink.

"But they were your dad's."

"I know. Over the years we were never together very much." She was referring to her and her sister with Roger and me. I noted her

183

choice of the past perfect tense. This was it. "We never really became a family. Keep 'em as something to remember me by."

"We only had a couple of Christmases, didn't we?"

"Yeah, and that's it! I always felt sad about that," she said.

I remembered that she had sent me a letter years before trying to get some form of personal or familial relationship started. Though her desires conformed to Dad's desire for Roger and me to be "one happy family" with Lil's crew, responding positively felt like opening to a risky form of entanglement I felt loathe to enter. I let the letter drop and never answered it. Content to keep the cufflinks, I thought it generous of her to give them to me.

We chatted lightly back and forth, Lil with Lynn and with Charlene, Roger with Gloria, me with Lynn mostly. Billy, across the table, seemed sullen. He was the spitting image of his father, whom Lil so disliked. He was square, grey, crude in his manner.

When Lil and Lynn left the table to circulate to the other tables, Billy's protective instincts for his sister, so unlike his father, showed themselves. "Was the removal of all that hardware your idea?" he blurted out suddenly.

I assumed he was referring to the lowering of the casket at the cemetery. "Yes, it was," I responded. I felt nervous because I could see his anger. His sister had been hurt, he thought. They probably had a conversation in the car.

"Whadja do that for?"

I was determined to rise above the steel in Billy's glare. That meant I needed to flip into teaching mode. "The Rite of the Christian Funeral, Bill, is built as a journey, a journey from the deathbed to the person's burial. The journey needs an end. Over the years I have found that families have ambivalent feelings, even some anxiety, about leaving a casket sitting up and out in an open field as they pull away, with no one there. Because of that, what we have done in the parish over the last few years is lower the casket. The rite is built for the lowering and the lowering is more satisfying for families because it brings things to a definite and realistic conclusion. Families find it helpful."

"What about kids?" he asked. I felt in the clear because he was approaching it from the point of view of intellectual curiosity. "You wouldn't do it if kids were there, wouldja?"

"Yes, Bill, we would. We have. Kids understand it. They are curious about it. They stand close, peer down into the grave and talk about it. Contrary to what you might think, lowering the casket helps with kids especially."

"I haven't seen that in I bet forty years."

"Well, we do it in Minnesota. When I asked Jeff Dames about it, he said it's done here to. I checked it out before I did it."

Lil was heading back to the table. From the look on Bill's face the conversation was over. I felt an instinctive dislike for him, glad our engagement had ended and grateful that I had taken the opportunity to approach it as a teachable moment rather than a defense at the ramparts.

●　　●　　●

Dad would often tell stories about Billy. He liked him, and Billy, though his Dad and Mom's favorite, felt protective of Lil. Father of four daughters, Billy owned a farm and did trucking work on the side. He kept a Lincoln Town Car in the barn. He was comfortable financially and Dad kept telling me that he would do anything he could for Lil. Dad and Lil saw Billy in Florida twice a year.

When Dad's Alzheimer's began, he and Lil considered whether they could remain in Florida or not. They thought their alternative might be to return to Illinois. As one of their options, they considered living in a place on Billy's farm.

During one Illinois trip while they were considering a move, they stayed out at the farm for a day. After lunch Billy invited Dad to help with something on the farm. Surprisingly, Dad said he declined. Then Dad said why. Ever the dandy, Dad was wearing white slacks and shoes with a red shirt and socks. The farm was mud. "I would never fit in a place like that," he said. "You can't even wear what you want. I'd never fit in a place where you had to wear overalls."

I never knew whether Dad told Lil his real feelings about the matter or evaded the issue. He spoke to me about the farm with disdain.

• • •

The one table I wanted to circulate towards was the one with the St. Joe's crowd so I could see Muggs Videtich. I walked over to say hello.

"You did a great job this morning, Father," Richard Churnovic said. He was a classmate of Dad's. His son, Ricky, was a classmate of mine, and his daughter, Lynn, a classmate of Roger's. "I don't know how you did that. I could never have done it," he said.

I thanked him, thinking he would be amazed if he knew the discussions of the past days and how I really felt about Dad. A couple of others said polite things. I thanked them, then squatted to talk to Muggs.

"Hey," she said. "We have been talking about this here. Why was the casket lowered?" She got right down to business with Father, avoiding chat with Michael.

"We lower the casket by custom in Minnesota," I responded.

"I wondered about that. We thought maybe that was it."

I then took the opportunity to do some teaching again. She accepted it well, as did the other folks at the table who were listening in.

"Had you ever seen that before?" I asked.

"Years ago," she said. "But not for, oh, maybe forty years."

I explained that Jeff had told me it was done in Joliet. That was news to all of them.

Abandoning hope of reaching beyond being Father to just being Mike, I got up and headed back toward our table. Gloria had a camera and wanted to record the event for posterity. As the picture taking with Roger, Gloria, Lil, and Lynn ended, Alex and Delores Plut walked over to me.

"I am sorry about last night, Fr. Mike," Delores said. "I didn't know what was going to happen until she got in the car, then what could I do? It was too late."

I explained to Delores and Alex about my encounter with Marge at Dad's grave, and that I took it as a good sign. Delores agreed with my assessment. They bade farewell with a promise to keep in touch.

As the exits went on, I caught Gloria by the side. "Hey, I have to drop Roger off at O'Hare later. Would you be interested in having supper at Merichka's afterward?"

"Why sure! I'd love to. What time?" We agreed on seven o'clock.

As Gloria and I walked to the door I saw Muggs flirting with Roger, teasing him about how young he looked. She asked me as I approached, "How's my good friend Mary Jean?"

Finally, the professional presentation could drop. Rog and I filled Muggs in on the essentials.

Before reaching the entryway, I turned to Lil and took her aside to say goodbye. "Thanks for everything. I hope you are okay."

"Yes, Michael, I am fine. Everything went very well, just the way he would like it. And I am so glad you lowered the casket at the grave. It was hard but it helped. Thank you." I wondered what the car conversation had really been, and what had happened since.

Rog and I got in the car and went back to the motel for a nap before the trip to O'Hare. Since we would have some extra time, I suggested that maybe we could stop by Dad's grave before leaving town. Rog was game. I asked if we could also buy a trowel so we could trim the stone at Grandma and Grandpa Papesh's grave since the stone was sinking and overgrown. He agreed. So, on the way to the motel we stopped at Builder's Square, then went to our motel room for a nap.

CHAPTER XII
Post Mortem

Rog and I both felt worn out but had little expectation of sleep. We hoped simply for rest and quiet. The interlude was helpful, especially considering the drive and flight for him and the drive, dinner with Gloria, and trek back to Minnesota the next day for me.

When we got up, he finished packing. I suggested we leave a little early since I wanted to get to the meal with Gloria on time. I also thought the traffic would be horrendous. Rog agreed.

We got to the cemetery about four o'clock. The grave was a brown mound with flower bouquets strewn on it. It felt strange to us both.

"You know what the funniest thing is for me, Rog? I have a greater sense of Dad's presence here at the grave than I did with his body."

"Me, too, Mike. It just didn't seem like Dad. Somehow I get a deeper sense that he is here."

We both squatted down and clumsily cut away the grass from Grandma and Grandpa Papesh's stone with the new trowel, then cleared the mud away by hand. The stone needed to be reset but now was not the time for that, since neither of us had the money.

We said goodbye to Dad, each in our own way, and drove to O'Hare. We talked some about the experience we had just been through and about Karen and the kids and what was happening in their lives. A restful, peaceful ride, the conversation aimed toward the future.

We arrived at O'Hare without delay because traffic was surprisingly light. I pulled into the lines at the United terminal, then stopped the car to let Roger out. I got out to open the trunk and he dove for his suitcases.

"You know, Roger, I want to say that I appreciated being with you very much during these days and I love you very much."

Rog instantly stopped, stood up and held his hands up over his head. "Ooooo-Ooooo!" he exclaimed, as if he was experiencing an exhilaration beyond words. "I have spent the last two days hugging all sorts of people, Mike, and you are the only one I have really wanted to hug."

With that he swooped me into a bear hug. "I love you, too."

He grabbed his suitcase from the trunk and headed into the terminal. I got back into the car and floated to Joliet for supper with Gloria.

I arrived at Gloria's a little early, but she was ready. I felt tired but looked forward to the time. She seemed, as always, game for anything. We drove to Merichka's, a Slovenian restaurant where we gathered as a family whenever I was in town these past many years. The place sat three blocks from St. Joe's cemetery.

When I asked her how she was doing, Gloria said that she was alright now that everything was over. Then I asked about the whole event. "How was all this for you?"

"Oh, Michael, I did just fine with it. I don't understand where Lillian was coming from for most of this, but I never did understand their way of life anyway. I am so glad you and Rog did right by your dad, though. He would have been proud of you." Her appreciation was heartening. She was the only person other than Mom and Rog who would have understood.

The waitress then came by and we ordered. After she left, Gloria went on. "You know, she called me and asked me what she should do."

"When?" I asked.

"After you called and said you wanted to buy a casket and bury him."

"Really?"

"Oh, yeah," she said, knowing that trouble lurked under the call.

"What did you say?"

"I tol' 'er, 'Hey, if they wanna spend the money, let 'em.'" The characteristic technique Gloria used with folks was to be blunt and cavalier, never letting on that she understood precisely the full lay of the land and, in fact, took the opposing side to the caller.

"Thanks, Gloria. I was relieved she said okay. It was touch-and-go, but I couldn't have imagined anything else for Dad."

"Me neither. You and Rog did right. Lil didn't understand."

"Gloria, do you know any details about Dad's death?"

"Boy, that was a source of a lot of tension, too."

"What happened?"

"Well, Tina called Lil at Lynn's and tol' 'er that the nursing home had called her and said Mickey wasn't doing very well. She went down to see him. He was pretty bad. So, she decided to call Lil to tell her that he was dying and that she should get down to Florida. Lil and Lynn both blew it off as Tina exaggerating. Lil felt really terrible about that when he actually died. That's why she was so mixed up there for a few days."

I both understood and felt a little resentful, especially since we were no part of the equation as his sons. "Did that call have anything to do with Tina's not coming."

"Sure. I guess there were words of some sort between 'em."

"Did Tina stay with Dad?"

"Yeah, she spent time with him. He was unconscious but she said he squeezed her hand a little bit at one point, so he knew she was there she thought."

"Wow! Isn't that sad, Gloria? The person who was with Dad when he died was Tina Bozich!"

"She wasn't there when he died. He died alone. But, yeah, it was really sad. What can you do?" Gloria was matter-of-fact about most family things. She had gotten used to letting go of events in all our lives, especially Dad's, because so little of it made sense to her. Little made sense to me, too.

Gloria then shifted subjects and began talking about the upcoming wedding of her daughter Jackie and the adjustment that was for her. Jeff, the prospective groom, was a good man, but their staying overnight together, leaving her alone in the apartment, bothered Gloria. At thirty-six, Jackie was free to do what she wanted but Gloria found it hard. To my surprise we talked about what might be most appropriate for Gloria in the situation, and she wanted that.

When the bill came, I took it and paid it. As we were gathering things together to go, I said, "Thanks, Gloria, for all you have done to offer us support through this. It has been a tough week or so. You have made a difference and I appreciate it."

"Oh, that's alright. What's family for?" she said with a big smile. "Besides, he would have been happy with how things turned out." She paused for a long moment, going deep within it seemed, then said with wonderment and deliberation, "You know, Michael, he was my brother and all, but he sure was mean."

•   •   •

Lil first noticed the possibility of Dad's Alzheimer's in October 1995 when he was sixty-nine. Dad lost his job as a funeral home manager then because he struggled with some memory and disorientation problems. The doctor had diagnosed the disease by the time I came to visit in January. Because of the progression we had seen in Grandma Papesh, we knew from the moment Alzheimer's was diagnosed that Dad's time would be limited.

I took a sabbatical during the first six months of 1998, staying at the Colorado ranch with Mom and Joe, doing spiritual reading for the duration. Since I had time, I thought it would be a good idea for Roger, the kids, and me to visit Florida together in spring during Easter break. Because Dad was failing, it struck me that we should be together one more time as a family and give the kids one last time – the second in Michael's life, the first in Kristen's – to be with their grandfather. I invited Gloria along as well. All said yes. Accidentally, we scheduled the gathering in Florida during a time when Lillian was planning to go to Illinois. Lillian appreciated our being with Dad while she traveled since she felt she needed the time away and with her family. Consequently, Roger, the kids, Gloria, and I stayed alone with Dad for six days.

On a Saturday afternoon, mid-week in our visit together, we decided to go to Mass. Since we all dressed up for Mass and it was a beautiful day, we decided to take a camera along so we could take some pictures of what was likely to be the last time we would all be together. The church sat next to a palm tree grove and lake, so the setting was ideally suited as a backdrop.

After Mass I got the family to stand and pose for the first picture. I noticed Dad had a cigarette in his right hand. Evidently, he lit up immediately after leaving Mass. I preferred to avoid leaving for posterity both the cigarette in Dad's hand and the limp-wristed gesture he used holding it. "Dad, would you mind putting the cigarette down for the picture."

"What, Son?" He was having trouble tracking what we were doing.

"The cigarette, Mick," Gloria said. "Mike wants you to put it down."

Dad hesitated. Gloria, standing at Dad's right and never one to hesitate, grabbed the cigarette from down at his side in his right hand and threw it into the grass.

Dad popped. "I'm hot! Wait a minute, I'm hot!" Dad was flushed red, very angry.

"Come on, Mick, just smile," Gloria said. "You can light-up later."

"I'm hot!" he said. We all waited, staring. He got the message. He managed to contain himself enough so I could snap the picture. After that he calmed.

Dad's temper, flashing and intense, always ignited over little things. I had an accident with his 1965 Cadillac Sedan de Ville when I was seventeen. I drove it immediately to the funeral home to tell him. He looked the car over, asked if it was drive-able, and when I said yes, he said, "Well, you may as well go to the party."

A dripping toothbrush or the lawnmower left in the yard, though, could cause a family conflagration. We always walked on eggs at home because of that.

I felt amazed that Saturday afternoon in Florida that three years into Alzheimer's disease, at seventy-two, Dad remained as touchy and flaring as ever about little things. Within that event I realized how terribly people around him spoiled Dad and let him have is way as he controlled us with his temper. Bequeathed his temper and always ill-at-ease with that, I resolved that day to work hard to let things go when my temper flashed, especially if my temper risked being demanding of others.

•   •   •

After the funeral, and once I was back in St. Paul, I called Mom and filled her in on the funeral and its aftermath. I also thanked Joe again for his financial help, which arrived in the mail the following day. The more I thought about it, the more amazed I felt that Joe, who had stolen Dad's wife, had helped pay for his casket.

I immediately went back to parish ministry rather than take time off. Summertime was ideal for a slow pace and rest since parishes, especially those with schools, abide in low key then. Added to that, in Minnesota people go to "the lake," which is how everyone describes their family cabin on any one of the of the 15,295 Minnesota lakes, for weekends and sometimes weeks at a time. For two weeks I napped, ate well, exercised with the dogs, and generally laid back.

CHAPTER XIII
Exploring Step-Reality

In mid-June I received a small cardboard box in the mail. The return address was Lil's. I cut it open to find ten ties and the crucifix from Dad's casket. No note had been included.

I focused especially on the ties. Dad had had a reasonably large collection of ties. One Lil sent I remembered from when I was a teenager. I had worn only the priest uniform for the last fifteen years, however, never a tie. Moreover, Dad tied his ties once, then hung them in his closet tied. The ties in the box, all rumpled at two places, had been untied without further ado. Mixed feelings crashed into one another as I beheld the ties. I decided to call Roger. "Hey, Rog, I got my inheritance today! Did you?"

"Oh, hi, Mike! Yeah. I got my inheritance, too. What did you get?"

"I got ten ties and the crucifix from Dad's casket."

"Oh, I got about twenty ties and the flag."

"Really! The ties are a mess, Rog. They're wrinkled and some are dirty."

"Yep, mine, too!"

"What are you going to do with the flag, Rog?"

"I have no idea! But I guess we can write anything else off, huh, Mike?"

We both laughed about Lil's attempt at thoughtfulness and at the uselessness of sending ties to a priest and to a casual-wear IBM technician who sported the childhood nickname Pigpen. We both knew we would have to delve into the inheritance question, but we held back from discussing it further right then.

A couple of days later, I called Lil to tell her I had received the package and to thank her. She told me that she was sorting through some of Dad's things and thought we might like to have some of his ties.

"The sorting must be hard, Lil."

"Yes, it is," she said with emotion. "But it has to get done."

"I hope you don't push yourself too hard. Take the time you need."

"Well, I have to. I am taking Dad's suits and things to a consignment shop to sell them and they only take two items at a time."

I was stunned. Dad's self-concept had no room for his wardrobe being publicly sold, much less sold piecemeal. "Really, Lil?"

"Yes. I got $15 each from two of his suit coats so far. I wish they would take more at once."

"Yeah, that must be hard to have the process so drawn out like that." I knew well that any money Dad had at the time of his death was thanks to Lil's saving. Dad believed that money was to be used not stashed and he enjoyed having a big car, nice things in the house, good clothes, and meals out. Though the nursing home and later Medicaid had forced the diminishment of their resources, selling the clothes of the dead still sounded less like frugality than bailing against the threat of penury. All I could do was let go.

I genuinely appreciated Lil's thoughtfulness and felt sincerely grateful for the crucifix. Her lack of tender care about the ties, and evident financial panic, however, surprised me.

In mid-August, I received another cardboard box in the mail. I opened it to find two silk robes. Pierre Cardin with three-quarter length sleeves; one was blue with white polka dots, the other burgundy with a paisley print. Both looked like Brooks Brothers ties exploded into a full garment.

Though freshly clean and fragrant, the robes spontaneously left me feeling anxious and repulsed. First, I had never owned a garment like them, nor imagined that I would or could. A flannel or cotton man by habit, I enjoyed snuggling up in my night clothes, preferring them homey warm. These garments, thin and light, felt like I remember Mom's night gowns feeling. Second, to my dismay, I associated the robes with sex.

Dad always fussed over Mom, kissing her and being flirtatious with her around the house, privately speaking to her about how beautiful and soft she felt to the touch. I gathered from watching and listening to him that sex was an extremely important, even necessary, experience in life and romance was a constant delight.

Mom, on the other hand, felt oppressed by Dad's constant preoccupation with sex and objectified and disrespected by his demands. I gathered from watching and listening to her that sex was relatively incidental in a relationship; it could even be exploitative, meaningless, and repulsive.

This set of double messages obtained after Mom and Dad divorced and remarried. Dad, bragging, once showed me a picture of himself on his fifty-fifth birthday clothed only in a red bikini silk bottom with a bull pictured on the crotch. Lil had gifted that to him. Mom, on the other hand, felt relieved at Joe's passivity about sex and his gradually becoming "incapable," as she put it. With both I squirmed in these conversations.

When we were children our bedroom door stood across a short hallway, the width of the bathroom door, from Mom and Dad's. Our bed was positioned so I could see right into their bedroom and bed, Dad's side especially. I remembered occasionally seeing Dad get up in the darkness and walk into the bathroom clad only in a sleeveless tee shirt with his hand covering his genitals. I never quite knew what was going on, but I was put off by it.

The two silk robes, elegant as they appeared to be as garments, struck me as outfits for sex, probably purchased for Dad by Lil, like the bull-crotched red shorts. I couldn't imagine wearing one of them with cotton pajamas, much less flannel. They seemed fashioned to be worn naked. I could imagine Dad in them, and how he used them. The robes evoked anxiety in me.

To add to my discomfort, and to my insistent impression that Lil just didn't get it, Lil put a note in the box this time. "I hope you can use the robes. Maybe you will feel closer to him." Too close to him was how the robes felt, too close! But what was I to do with them? I called Roger. "Hey, I got another piece of my inheritance today. Did you get a box?"

"No, Mike, I didn't. What did you get?"

I explained and, though embarrassed, told him my associations. He shared them. Then I asked, "Do you want 'em?"

"Hell, no!" he said. "What am I going to do with them?"

"How about Michael?" He was eighteen. "Could Michael use them?"

"No. He would only use them as an outfit for sex. No. Bad idea."

"Rog, what can I do with them?"

"Well, wait a minute here, Mike. Maybe there's something in this for you. You're the one who believes that God does things to make a point. Maybe there's something in these for you. Keep them. Wear them. See what's in it for you."

"Rog, you're serious?" My anxiety surged. It had never occurred to me to put one on.

"Yeah, Mike. I think you should hang onto them and see what's up."

"How do you mean that?" I loved pulling his leg.

"Not that, Mike! You know what I mean."

Intrigued, I decided to follow Roger's lead. So, several nights later, after a shower and before I put my pajamas on for bed, I put one of the robes on to say night prayer. The garment was light and soft, very comfortable, rich even. Nonetheless, I decided I couldn't keep it. Though the robe covered me completely, I felt exposed in it. So, I decided to give the robes to the parish maintenance coordinator if he would take them. He took them and appreciated having them.

I decided to call Lil to thank her, though, before I gave them away. When I called, Lil said what her note said, that she hoped the robes would help me feel closer to him. She also shared that she was continuing her clothing sales and missing Dad very much, too.

"I have also placed the order for the gravestone," she said.

"Oh! What did you get?" I asked, instantly on high alert. With her once again charging ahead without Roger and me, I felt internally shut down, fearing the answer.

"I am getting it from the Veterans Administration. It will be a bronze plaque."

"Oh, that will be nice," I responded blandly. I was furious.

Dad rarely spoke of his time in the service and he would bristle against the idea of his grave marker being a free bronze plaque bolted to a cement slab. His sense of himself demanded granite and, even though flush to the ground, a gravestone that matched the family graves. That was precisely what he did for his parents, what he certainly would have wanted. I decided, however, not to argue. There would come a day, I knew, when that plaque would have to be replaced.

"I am sending you a picture, too, Michael. It was the last one taken of your dad," she said. "And it's a good one," she added with emphasis.

"Thanks, Lil, I am looking forward to it. I will be glad to have it."

Within days, in fact, I received the snapshot from Lillian, and two from Gloria. The one Lil sent had been taken in December 2000. The two Gloria sent were the infamous pictures taken by the Sczepaniaks February 27 and March 1, 2001. In Lil's, Dad was tidy, if serious. The Sczepaniak pictures showed Dad with his left upper lip raised slightly, clearly annoyed, perhaps confused. Gloria's pictures looked truer to Dad than Lil's did.

Eventually, the packages stopped coming. I remained mindful, though, that we needed to do something about asking for things we would like to have either from our grandparents, or their parents, or from our life as a family pre-divorce. In January 2002, I asked Roger about it.

"It's been seven months, Rog. I call her every six weeks or so to say hello, but she has said nothing. What do you think we should do?" I asked.

"Wait until she dies, Mike."

"What? Really?"

"Yeah. I think it will be easier dealing with the girls than dealing with Lil. Besides, by then, it won't matter much."

"But, Rog, will we even be in touch with her by then?" I wondered about that because keeping relationship with Lil felt strained and required work. Lil took no initiative whatsoever but for the packages. My calls were growing farther and farther apart.

"Who knows?" he responded. "Probably. We'll have to be."

I felt ill-at-ease with his response but decided to let it go for now. Following whatever instinct would eventually arise seemed likely the better way to handle this question anyway.

Instinct struck in a phone call to Lil on March 10. Lil seemed sad, not herself, when the conversation began. As it went along, she perked up.

"Are you going to Jackie's wedding in April, Lil?" Jackie, Gloria's daughter, was marrying for the first time. I couldn't be there because it was First Communion weekend in the parish. Roger lived too far away. Because I thought her friends with Gloria, I expected Lil would probably go.

"No, Michael, I'm not. I am traveling to Biloxi just a few days later, and it would be too much."

I felt surprised, especially at the reasoning. I had always thought of family first, no matter what. "What's in Biloxi, Lil?"

"Oh, gambling!" she said with glee. "A friend of mine and I went up there last year and it was fun. This time we are going to fly."

"That sounds like fun," I said. My Irish was roused, however. She was, in my view, pulling back from the family to "do her own thing," as Dad would say. On top of that, a woman who was selling her late husband's clothes was planning to fly to Mississippi to gamble. It flashed in me instantly that now was the time to talk inheritance, because inheritance was now or never. Besides, it had been almost ten months.

"Oh, by the way, Lil. When we were together back in May 1998, you mentioned that Roger and I should compile a list of some things we might want in memory of Dad. I have talked to Roger and we have a list. I am wondering how we should proceed on this. Do you want to see it? Do you want to wait? What do you think?" I decided to start easy.

"Well, I don't know," she said with audible anxiety. Then with a little tension, hinting of anger, she said, "I haven't thought about it."

She sent ties and robes but hadn't thought about it? I decided to press on. "Lil, would it be helpful for you to have the list? I don't want to read it over the phone or anything like that, but might I send it to you?"

"I don't know." Clearly, I had caught her off-guard and was skating on thin ice. "Did you have the white cross put on the grave?" she blurted out with heat. "My mother was there, and she said a white cross was on the grave."

"No, Lil, I didn't." I finally saw a glimmer of the reality underneath all her passivity and niceness: resentment and defensiveness, as I had supposed. "I was there in September." I had gone down for Gloria's 70th birthday and had enjoyed a Merichka's poorboy at Dad's grave with him and the family. "The cross was there then. I assume it typical cemetery practice to place a cross until the tombstone arrives."

"Well, I was wondering. The stone should be there in June."

"Oh, that's great," I responded mildly. But being grimly determined on my goal, like my father, I had to try again. "Lil, what about the issue of Roger and I having some things, like you suggested in 1998?" Deep inside I felt shaken, so decided to go for broke. "Actually, there's a second issue, too. Dad told me he left a will and we would like to see it. But for now, since we talked about leaving the money alone, what about our having some things?"

"I don't know," she said. She seemed to snap and move toward shutting down. "I have to think about it." That remark aimed to close discussion.

"Lil, would a list help you think about it?" I felt as if this was our last chance, so I pushed all the way. All the while I realized I didn't trust her. I also realized in a flash that I didn't trust Dad and what may have transpired between them. I remained nice, but intrepid, trying to shield the darkness within. "Then you would know what we are asking. Can I send the list?"

"Yes, you can send the list," she said, defeated. We continued the call briefly, chatting until I sensed a bit of cheer. Then we hung up.

I called Mom and Roger right away.

"Boy, did she ever find out that Mickey was not dead when she talked to you!" Mom said after hearing the story.

True. I inherited his apologetic persistence. Like Dad, Roger could go round-and-round saying nothing. I failed at that. I always carried courteous doggedness, polite relentlessness, and sweet stubbornness in my quiver for shooting when I needed them.

"The other thing is, Mike, that I am glad you are doing this. I thought you had better not wait. The relationship won't last. It's now or never."

"I thought so, too," I rejoined. "I can't see how we are going to stay in touch over the years. She's pulling back from the family already."

When I got through to Roger two days later, he seemed taken aback that I had raised the issue. "Mike, she can be really awful, you know."

"Like Tina, you mean?"

"Yes, just like Tina. She can be tough. I guess we'll see what happens."

I then went through a list with him, and we agreed on the items and the distribution. We had discussed the list several times in the past anyway. I wrote it the day Lil and I talked four years before and had been adding, subtracting, and modifying it since. It took little time to refine the list.

"Mike, make sure you tell her what these things are, why we want them."

"That will drive her nuts, Rog."

"Yep. That's the point," he said with a chuckle.

"She'll probably want to throw some of the things out the door when I write her about where they come from and why we want them."

"That's just what we want," he said.

"Okay. You've got it!"

15 March 2002

Dear Lil,

Enclosed is the list of things Roger and I have agreed that we would like to have as mementos of Dad, our forebears and of our family life during our growing-up years. I am offering it to you in the spirit in which we spoke at the McDonald's back in May 1998, when you suggested we do such a list. At that time, you spoke about money being minimal, but suggested that if we wanted some things to remember Dad by, that would be fine. I accepted that at face value and agreed then to do a list. This letter has it.

Raising the subject on the phone March 10 was awkward for me. I gather it was for you, too. I know things like this create stress and tension in all families. I expect they stir up in you grief and a wide array of emotions. The same is true for Roger and me. I am sorry, though, for whatever stress and tension this causes you. However, it is only reasonable that this be done. I also know no other way to proceed with this kind of concern than to be direct about it and give you the time you need to think about it. So, I see our asking for some things as consistent with our conversation of four years ago, respectful of your financial need, and a natural, normal, ordinary part of our desire to have things around us and for future generations that remind us where we came from, spark stories and commemorate family members and events. I am sorry if the process is painful.

Here's what Roger and I have agreed about asking for. As you know, sentiment is unfathomable mystery. Please understand, too, that as we offer this list, Rog and I will certainly accept full responsibility for packing, shipping, and expenses. I also assume that one or both of us will likely need to come down to make arrangements, etc. We ask nothing of you, only a sense of "when" and guest accommodations when the time comes.

Here are the items:

- **Black/blue .38 pistol**
  This was used by Grandpa Papesh and Clark Hously for security at the tavern. Roger already has the silver gun. He would like this one, too.
- **Gold pocket watch**
  This belonged to Uncle Ignatius Papesh. Dad and he were each other's favorites. Ignatius left it to Dad when he died in 1944.
- **Gold chain attached to the watch**
  This chain, with a little pearl setting in it, belonged to

Aunt Nell Jordan, our great-grand aunt. Mom attached it to the watch sometime in the late sixties and wore it for many years.

- **Painted pewter lamp**

  This lamp, which Dad touched-up in Florida, was in the center of the dining room table at Ruby Street. It was in your living room on the record cabinet when I last saw it.

- **Brass and marble table**

  This table belonged to Grandpa Papesh's mother, Mary Perko Papesh. Dad had it plated in 1959. He was all excited about that, as was Roger, who was seven years old and with Dad when he got the work done. It was in your dining room.

- **Salt cellar**

  This belonged to Grandma Papesh. It was in the dining room breakfront.

- **Glassware (storage dish, pitcher, glasses)**

  These belonged to Grandma Papesh and were in the breakfront.

- **Silver sugar spoon with "Mother" engraved in it and silver matching butter knife**

  These items, which you have used daily, belonged to our maternal great-great grandmother in South Elgin, Mary Jordan, born in Ireland.

- **Dark colored framed painting with woods and bridge and bible stand with black marble top**

  These were a gift to Dad from Ernie Wunderlich, Dad's mentor and best friend for years. They came from Ernie's funeral home.

- **Bible**

  Roger and I gave it to Mom and Dad as their twenty-fifth wedding anniversary gift.

- **China**
  Dad stood in line for twelve hours in 1945 in Japan to get this china. It was his engagement gift to Mom. We used it for all family holidays throughout our growing up years. The gravy boat broke on the trip to Florida, otherwise it was fully intact as a set.
- **White linen table cloth with matching napkins**
  Dad gave this to Mom for their tenth wedding anniversary in 1956.
- **Burgundy glass vase with clear glass flowers and pedestal**
  This was a wedding gift to Mom and Dad from Mom's aunt.
- **Red bird with blue base**
  Dad would show-up at home with things he saw and liked. This bird – he was proud that the beak never broke – he came home with in the spring of 1960.
- **Dining room brass and glass chandelier**
  Rog and I would be happy pay for the installation of a new one. The chandelier is from Cowles Avenue and was there when we moved in on March 15, 1958 – forty-four years ago today, in fact. Along with Grandma Papesh's brass table, Dad had this plated through a friend of Larry Ryan's and was very excited about it. Larry was too. Roger was there for the plating.
- **Gold (roses and rope) glass topped table**
  This table went with the original living room furniture Mom and Dad picked out in 1963 up at John M. Smythe in Chicago. We were all always especially attached to it. It was the object of several family jokes, for instance it was called the "welder's nightmare."
- **Brass reading lamp**
  This lamp, which we last saw in your guest bedroom on

the south, Roger took apart for a babysitter when he was five. It marks the beginning of his permanent devilment with tools and such.

- **Steel lantern lamp and large magnifying glass**
  These two items came from John Coyle, a friend of Roger's during his high school years. The lamp was in the back bedroom.

- **Records**
  We would like to have the Beatles (two or so), Beach Boys, Four Seasons (one), Shelley Berman (two), Monkees (one), *Reader's Digest Classics* set, *Montovani in Italy*, and the forty-five rpms (with the plastic post adjusters) from the 1960s. These were the music of our childhood and teen years.

- **Cuff links**
  I have several pairs of Dad's cuff links. I would be happy to have any left. I wear them several times a week.

- **White, gold, and pink ceramic V-shaped accent lamp with lid and pink and white glass hurricane lamp with gold and flowers**
  These are both items that Dad picked up in the late fifties when we first moved to Cowles Ave.

- **Family photos up to 1974**
  We simply would like to have the whole family record.

- **Living room French Provincial furniture**
  We assume you need this for now but ask that you re-member us whenever it is you decide to dispose of it. We will, of course, move it. Specifically, we mean the love seat, couch, two fire side chairs, flower-patterned side chair, red velvet side chair, matching incidental tables, record cabinet, barrel table, tall, white and brass lamp, and wall sconce. These items, which Mom and Dad pur-chased between 1963 and 1970 in Chicago, we were espe-

cially proud of – and it took them a long time to find pieces Mom was satisfied with. The furniture was the only new furniture we ever saw, and it marked something of Dad's "coming into his own" professionally. Roger traveled with them in Chicago as Mom and Dad shopped.

I would also like to raise the thorny question of the will. Dad told me back in 1996 while we were standing in the kitchen that he had one prepared. I think you were there, in fact. He made a point of letting me know that everything was taken care of, everything specified. We would very much like to have a copy of the will so we can honor his wishes in any particular distributions and so we can have the family record. For now, Roger and I have agreed between ourselves, with complete concord, on who gets what.

Thanks for considering this. I imagine it is even harder for you than for us. But I hope that the list itself, now, will take some of the anxiety out of it for you. We look forward to hearing from you or talking with you about all this and starting to sort through what it would take to make arrangements.

I indicated at the bottom that Roger would get a copy.

I ran the letter by Mom and Roger. Both agreed that it was direct but showed understanding. They approved. Reviewing the list with them and alone, I came to realize that Lil had lived for twenty-five years with furniture, paintings and jewelry that had deep associations for us and for Mom, but she probably knew nothing about where these things came from or what they meant. That realization took Dad down a notch in my esteem.

I decided to wait a while before calling Lil about the list. Thinking she likely would be angered by it, yet not wanting to place undue pressure, I decided to wait to call her until the Spirit moved me. Because spring can be a bracing time of year in a parish, I wanted to feel reasonably balanced and sure when I called, especially since I would be getting who-knew-what in response. So, I confined my communication with her to the regular dutiful exchanges. She received my weekly homilies and the weekly parish bulletin. I sent her a card at Easter, on Mother's Day, on her birthday in May. I received nothing back. Since that was not unusual, I let it go.

May 31 marked the first anniversary of Dad's death. I felt obliged to call Lil that day. It was a Friday and I felt sick with a cold and migraine. So, I called Lil on Saturday June 1, late morning.

"Hi, Lil. Michael."

"Oh, hi, Michael." I could tell that she was in a tired and crabby mood. I decided to avoid the letter.

"Since yesterday was Dad's anniversary, Lil, I thought I would give you a call. I was sick yesterday, though, so I called today. How are you doing?"

She told me that her younger daughter, Tina, was moving. She was sorting through Tina's things, lifting boxes, and generally helping her out. She had only stopped home for a sandwich and a break. We talked about Tina's new place briefly. She was stressed. Lil lived stressed it seemed.

"I also heard from Gloria that you lost your job?" I framed it carefully as a question.

"Well, I didn't lose it," she snapped back. "They had to close the store." She explained that the owner was ill and needed to close shop because of it. "I am taking the summer off, and then I will see what I need to do."

"Oh, good for you." She was caring for herself, though I surmised she still needed to work.

Then Lil made a sudden turn. "I have been very mad at you. I suppose you know. I have been thinking of calling you but haven't wanted to."

I had no expectation she would call. Even in the case of death she only left a message. Moreover, how would I know she was mad, particularly very mad? I felt nervous, wholly unsure about the lay of the land with her. Nonetheless we were on. "What have you been mad about?" I asked blandly.

"That letter you sent with the list in it. I didn't need to know the history of everything and where everything came from. The list would have been just fine. It really hurt me. I knew all those things."

I didn't believe that for an instant but felt constrained to play the diplomat. We had never argued before. "I'm sorry, Lil, I didn't mean to hurt you. I didn't know what you knew or didn't know. I included the background simply so you would understand why we were interested in those things. It was just an effort to be clear."

"Well those things are mine. I have lived with them for twenty-three years. I know where they came from. You're telling me about your mom and their shopping together for these things… I didn't need to hear all that." She felt as touchy about Mom as Mom felt about her, I gleaned. I had never been sure.

"I simply didn't know that, Lil. I just wanted to be clear." I decided to be bland and just listen.

"And then telling me where they were in the house, as if I didn't know. I am not stupid, you know." Oops! Her psychology was more complicated than I knew.

"I am sorry, Lil. I did that to be clear. A lamp is a lamp is a lamp. I specified which ones so you would know what I meant. I am my father's son. I know where things are and what they look like in detail. I just wanted to be clear."

"And then you asked about the will. I want you to know that I went to a lawyer, and he said that you are not entitled to see anything. Why would you ask for a will?"

Her objecting was incomprehensible to me on one level. On another I felt sure that Lil had had a new will done after Dad had fallen deep into Alzheimer's. Attempting to confirm my suspicions and call an uncomfortable question, I had hoped to be indirect about it. "Because I knew Dad had done one. I am family, Lil. I am his son. I carry his name. I am his blood. The will is a public document. I feel obliged to respect his wishes. That's why I asked for the will."

"Well, he did a will in 1981, and there he gave you three things and Roger three things. I will send you that. He did another will in 1995. He doesn't specify any things in that will."

"This is the first I have heard that, Lil. I simply didn't know."

"The things here are mine and they will be till I die. I can saw their legs off if I want."

I sparked into a boil. I had long known a moment would come that would strip to nakedness the reality underneath our ritual niceness. We had arrived. "So, you are telling me that Roger and I will get nothing. Is that what you are saying?"

"No, I can distribute these things anytime I want. You are not going to empty my house of furniture and leave me with nothing."

"Lil, the letter doesn't say that." Clearly emotion trumped text for Lil and her negative bias shut down the possibility of negotiation or thoughtfulness.

"He told me when we did this will, 'I know my boys and they will pull in with a truck and empty you out.'" There it was! Lil was parroting Dad's hurt and anger and had made it her own. The grave in Joliet had flipped open and I had just heard the lament of the dead. "I had forgotten he said that," she went on. "Until I got this list. I could imagine you here with a clipboard and the list. When I read it, it reminded me of your grandmother."

I found that a low blow tactic, though typical of a family fight. Still, I felt confused by it. "What do you mean?"

"I mean your other one," she said referring to Mom's mother. Grandma Foster, nosy and enjoying the soap opera, had made anonymous, listening phone calls to the house while Dad and Lil were dating and during their early marriage until Dad called her back once and caught her. The reference was off-the-mark. Grandma Papesh would stand with the clipboard and note every item. Grandma Foster simply enjoyed the fight. Still, no ammunition was off-limits, evidently.

"Lil, if you think that, you misread the letter." I retreated from the emotional into the rational. I hoped it would cool things down. "I said specifically that when you want to get rid of the furniture, please think of us. I would never empty your living room of furniture."

"I have been so mad at you." Then she said, with emphasis, "I talked with my girls. They aren't attached to these things. They don't want these things. They have furniture of their own." The stew had been thickened, but that mattered little to me at this stage.

"I simply didn't know, Lil."

"When I die you can have this stuff. I have kept it up. I probably should have had it reupholstered. It's old. They don't want it."

"I appreciate that, Lil. That's all I asked." I hope we were moving toward reason. Perhaps holding back had paid off.

"And then those spoons and all that little stuff? I have put the list in a lock box, so you can have these things when I die."

"Thanks, Lil. I appreciate your offering me that assurance, that we can have those things eventually. That's all I ask. That's fine." I was utterly sincere and internally letting go. I had made my point and she honored it. I could ask nothing more.

"When we talked in 1998, I thought you just wanted a chair or something like that. I said you could have that. You even offered a couple of hundred dollars for it and I said, 'Why would you do that? No. Take it.'"

"Lil, we remember that conversation differently." Her ears and mine may have been wired that day to hear what we wanted to hear but I had crossed my Ts and dotted my Is about what I had heard. "I keep a diary. I began the list that day. I talked with Roger about it over the years, most recently before I sent it to you. I did that because I understood you expected it."

"Your father would never have approved of your sending me this," she said with meaning. He did treat her like a queen, and she did come to expect it. It was his way with both his wives.

"I simply don't know, Lil," I responded, avoiding the issue. I knew she was right. He always chose his wife over his sons.

"He would not have liked this list at all. And Roger would never want this furniture. What would he do with it? He wouldn't want it, would he?" She favored Roger and thought him funny.

Roger had expressly asked for the furniture and I had written so. Again, I avoided it with a blandly factual response. "Roger and I did the list together, Lil."

"When you called me, it had only been nine months. I was confused. I hadn't given these things any thought."

I felt heat again. "What do you mean, Lil? Roger and I each got a box of ties and I got a box of robes. Clearly you were thinking about these things."

"What was I going to do with that stuff? I had to get rid of it." She was avoiding the point and wisely so.

"And you agreed that I send the list, Lil. I asked and you agreed. I waited nine months to ask. For most families, these things happen long before that. I am just trying to do what I can when I can, following your lead, that's all. All of this is ordinary stuff in families. It's painful and filled with tension, and it is for all families. But I sent the list in an effort to be clear, Lil, and you consented to that." I refused to give my ground, though I felt self-conscious about having pushed.

"Well sometimes what you write isn't taken the way you think it will be when you write it." The runway was being foamed for a landing. I felt grateful.

"I know, Lil. And sometimes inner noise keeps a reader from seeing the words that are there. Besides, Lil, if you had been clear about what the will says when I talked with you March 5, we wouldn't be here today. If I had known then that no things were specified that would have been helpful." That was a ruse and defensive.

"The will talks only about the house," she said. "When I die and its sold, the proceeds are to be split four ways. That's all it says. The

1981 will mentions things. I can send you that." We were in the final approach for landing.

"Lil, I don't ever want, or need, to see the 1981 will. I know it has no legal standing. But if I had known in March, Lil, what the 1995 will says, this conversation would be different today. Still, I appreciate your willingness to respect our requests. That's all I ask." I decided to land, grateful for the foamed runway.

"You'll just have to wait, that's all."

"I understand, Lil. That's fine. I don't need anything more than that." At least I knew where we stood. Her family was long-lived, but at least some family things from the Papeshes might get to Roger's children and grandchildren.

"Well, okay." She ended it.

"Now it's back to moving Tina?" I asked. We finished the conversation in another five minutes or so with pleasantries and ease.

Two themes encouraged me heartily. First, she seemed to assume a basic loyalty to Dad and to us, even though she felt frustrated and had talked with a lawyer to understand her rights. I appreciated the loyalty. Second, and as a subset of the first, I gathered that Roger and I were still family for her, even if that reality was attenuated. Her assumption that we would be around and connected at the time of her death underlined that.

I also came away feeling discouraged about Dad. His assumption that we would empty the house on Lillian was typical of him. His whole life he took care of his wife first, failing to defend or trust Roger and me, to the point that he assumed the worst. I considered feeling hurt about that but decided instead to just try to be open to that ugly reality and accept it. After all, Dad's attitude underneath Lil's words, though rising out of the grave, held no surprise. It was simply more of the same.

About a month after our telephone conversation, I received a box in the mail from Lillian. I immediately assumed that it was yet another portion of my inheritance and wondered if she had perhaps had second thoughts. I opened it to find four pages of a 1970s photo album that displayed pictures of the inside of the Glenwood Avenue house. Underneath I found eight pictures of me and two pictures of a Porsche that Roger had owned. The box also held five video tapes, three Roger had done years before in order to share pictures of his family and new house with Dad and Lil, and two from a series of homilies I had video-taped a decade earlier for the Archdiocese. Topping off the contents, Lil had enclosed four shoeshine brushes – two brown, two black – which had come from Dad's kit.

I felt hurt and confused. I threw the brown shoeshine brushes away immediately because I owned no brown shoes and never would. I then called Roger and Mom.

Roger suggested that perhaps Lillian was being thoughtful. The box's contents were not all that bad. After all, I had asked Lil for pictures and we had learned to shine shoes with those brushes. When I reminded him that eight pictures and two videotapes of me were there, he said, "Oh, oh! It sounds like she doesn't want to have anything to do with you at all." That was my own considered reaction precisely.

Mom immediately got the very same message we did when I reported the contents to her. "Mike, it's over," she said.

"What do you mean?" I wanted to be clear.

"She doesn't want to have anything to do with you. Just forget it. Forget her."

That felt too easy. "Mom, I can't."

"Why not?" I could hear that her Irish was up a bit.

"Mom, though I may not like it very much, she is my step-mother. She will get at least cards from me for the rest of her life."

"Mike, why bother?"

"Well, Mom, I look at it this way. When she dies at least they will know my address."

I saw Roger in mid-June at Mom's place in Colorado and the subject of our inheritance rose again. He had spoken with Lil. "I tried to explain, Mike, that you think about family history, you're sentimental and all that. She's Slovenian. She's not there. Lil lives in today only. Look at the house. She had parents, a brother, and lots of nieces, aunts, and cousins. She has no family souvenirs or heirlooms. There's nothing. She doesn't think that way at all." His observations were illuminating.

"Not at all?" I asked.

"Not at all. Besides, you must remember, Mike, that Lil is in survival mode. She's worried even about food. She and Dad had their fun. He got off easy. He had fun, went wacky, then died. She's left with a small monthly pension and a dwindling little pile of money. Nothing was invested. There were no brains there. She's surviving. That's all"

I felt still ill-at-ease, looking for a clarity I failed to see. "So, what do you think, Rog, is going to happen with the things I asked about?"

"We'll get a call twenty years from now and it will all be out on the front lawn. Then, under pressure, we'll have to decide what to do. The moving guys, who make a killing in that kind of situation, will charge us $25,000 to move anything at all. Then we'll say, 'Get rid of it,' and take two suitcases of stuff home. That's it. That's the end of it."

I thought him coldly realistic, and right, but had to check again. "Really Roger, that's it?"

"Yeah, unless she moves into a condo back in Illinois. Then we might have a chance. But I don't think that's going to happen."

Mom, sitting by, chimed in, "Why don't you just forget about her?"

"Mom, she put in twenty-five years with Dad," Rog responded. "We owe her something for that."

CHAPTER XIV
The Dictates of Grief

On September 8, 2002, I decided to call Roger to check in because I had not spoken with him since mid-summer. I hit the speed dial and waited. The phone rang, then, "He-e-llo-o?"

The voice was female, weary, and unfamiliar. "Who Is this?" I asked.

"Lil," she said.

"Oh, Lil!" I felt flustered. I had hit the wrong button. "How are you?"

"Oh, I am fine," she said wearily.

I looked at my watch. "Lil, it's a quarter after ten at night. You were in bed, weren't you?"

"Yes."

"I am sorry I hit the speed dial and hit the wrong button. I would never call you so very late."

"That's okay."

"How are you?"

"Oh, I'm fine. I have been busy with the house, but other than that I am not doing too much. How are you, Michael?"

"I'm fine, too. The parish is doing better. Money is coming in. At the end of this month I have been asked to go to Cleveland to speak with three hundred priests about clerical culture. I am excited about that."

"That's nice." There was a lull. I groped for something.

"How are the girls, Lil?"

"They're fine. Lynn is doing her thing. Tina is sick, though."

"Oh, I'm sorry. I hope it's nothing serious."

"It is serious, but she'll take care of it."

"Oh, okay." Again, a lull. "Well, I am sorry, Lil, for calling you so very late. I am glad I caught you, but I am sorry for waking you up. I hit the wrong button here."

"Oh, that's okay."

"Well, you take care, Lil."

"Okay. Bye."

I was mortified that I had awakened her. She struggled with insomnia. Ambushed by the misdial, I had been unprepared to speak with her. I sensed her reluctance to get into anything either. Given the hour, I didn't know what to make of it at all and let it go.

On September 24, sorting my mail I found letter from Lil. When I opened the envelope, two pieces of paper fell out. One was a white, blue-lined, and red-margined, five-and-a-half by eight-and-a-half sheet. A note was written on it. The other piece of paper was a scissors-cut, plain white strip with a little rectangle of newspaper taped to its bottom. The taped piece was an obituary. It was Tina Bozich's, Lil's younger daughter. She had died September 14, ten days earlier. The hand-written note read:

9/20/02

Michael:

Your dad was very good to both my girls and they were good to him. They never forgot him on his birthday and holidays. Tina took care of him so I could keep my job.

Please notify Roger – I can't talk to anyone right now.

Lil

I felt stunned. Tina was forty-eight. I also felt taken aback that I was learning about it ten days after her death and being instructed that Lil wanted a communications embargo in place. I called Roger.

"She says nothing about the cause of death, Rog. What do you think it could be?"

"Mike, it could be a drug overdose. It could be suicide. Either of those could follow on what Lil shared with you earlier in the month. Tina lived a rough life. There are a lot of options."

When I met Tina in 1975, she appeared to be a tough high school student who wore tank tops with no bra, smoked pot, and slept around. As the years passed nothing much changed. She had lived in Illinois, California, and Hawaii, and she had died in Florida. At one point, while she was telling Dad and Lil that she worked for the United States Postal Service, Roger reported she had told him she was working the streets. The last time I saw her she was forty-two. A lanky bleached blonde smoking a cigarette, Tina wore a white tank top with no bra, a wisp of shaggy denim at the waist that passed for shorts, and black suede, laced platform boots that stopped just under her knees. She was living with an unnamed man who was out at the time and unacknowledged by Dad or Lil, even though we stood in her apartment and could plainly see evidence of him. Dad's easy pleasantness with her nonetheless, especially since he was such a straight arrow, surprised me.

"Should I call Lil, Rog?"

"No, Mike. I'd let it go. There's something going on here and she wants you out. Stay out."

I followed Roger's advice and sent a warm sympathy note to convey Roger's and my condolences.

In early October, I called Aunt Gloria to say hello. She reported that Tina's ashes had been brought up from Florida to Joliet and there was a graveside service for her. Gloria had been there.

"Guess what, Mike?" I could hear she felt unsettled. "She was buried next to your dad!"

"What?" I exclaimed. The news was incomprehensible.

"I guess Lil didn't want to spend any money, so Tina's ashes were buried in Lil's grave next to your dad."

I was amazed by what I regarded as the patent lack of manners. "You'd think they would ask, or talk about it, or something! I've heard nothing."

"Yeah, I know," Gloria said. "I was invited last minute. I don't like it but what can you do?"

When I told Rog the news his response was straightforward, "Well, Mike, there's no surprise there. Lil has no money and the grave was there."

"But isn't it astonishing that she didn't extend us the courtesy of asking us or even informing us?"

"Mike, that didn't occur to Lil. She was only thinking about money and herself." That blunt assessment rang true.

During Eastertime in 2002, Gloria telephoned to let me know that the Veterans Administration bronze marker had been installed on Dad's grave.

"How does it look, Gloria?"

"Well, he wouldn't have liked it."

"I know. What's on it?"

"It's got his name and the birth and death dates, and it says on top 'beloved husband.'"

"That's it?" My ears whistled with steam.

"Yep. I'll send you a picture. Isn't it a shame?"

I resolved instantly to take matters into my own hands but decided to call Roger before proceeding.

Roger's response was matter of fact. "Mike, we don't count for much to her anyway."

"Rog, we have been cut out of our own family's plot! That's the issue for me. This this cannot stand." I explained to him that I wanted to have a marker made up that matched the Papesh graves and have it installed in place of the bronze one. Besides Dad's name and the birth and death dates, I thought it ought to say three things: Mickey, funeral director, and father.

"Yep. I agree with that, Mike. He always gave his wife priority over us, but we are his legacy, not Lil. That's the right thing to do."

"Will you split the cost with me, Rog?"

"Sure, no problem. But you have to remember, Mike, this will be the end of things with Lil."

"Rog, she bypassed us through the funeral, was silent about Tina and burying her in the Papesh plot, and now has excluded us from our family graves. What else is there?"

"I'm okay with it, Mike, but you just have to remember."

I knew Roger was probably right. Still, larger family identity and history issues deserved respect.

•   •   •

In April 1998, when Roger, Michael and Kristen, Gloria and I descended on Dad in Florida, we had fun, told stories, ate out and toured the area. Because of his Alzheimer's, the week was hard on Dad, harder than we knew.

Roger and the kids went to the airport one day. Gloria was scheduled to fly out the next. During the night in-between, about 2:30 A.M. Dad came and knocked on my bedroom door. "Mike, Mike, are you there? Mike?"

Groggy, I responded, "Yeah, Dad?"

"Could you come out here? My mind broke."

I leapt out of bed. We walked together to the kitchen. There, standing at the counter, he tried to explain that he had gotten up to urinate, spit into the toilet as he did so, and then… well… he just couldn't put it together.

I listened to him, realizing that he probably had had a slight stroke in the process and hallucinated something regarding spittle and the toilet. He could not bring the story together. I felt sad for him. This experience showed me the kind of Alzheimer's he suffered: a series of small strokes extended over years until the stroke came that ended his life. I tried to comfort Dad, and it took forty-five minutes for him to calm down. Then I put him to bed.

As I fell back to sleep, I felt pleased that I was the one he asked for help, the one he trusted. I felt affirmed and humbled.

•　　•　　•

Because I wanted to remain within my rights on the matter, I decided to begin the grave marker process with Jeff Dames. After explaining the situation, he said he had some research to do, then he would call me back.

"Well, Father, this is the law," Jeff reported a day later. "The eldest son inherits the rights over the graves of the family plot. He owns them. So, as a matter of law, you can do what you wish. However, Lillian has the rights to her grave and the right to extend her grave to another. Your father effectively granted her that. She has exercised her legal rights in extending the grave to Tina's ashes, but that also means that she will be able to use the grave herself only if she is also cremated."

"That's quite likely, Jeff."

"Well, Father, we need to see what happens there. But you have the right as the eldest son to do what you wish with your father's marker. Lillian has no rights she can legally exercise except over her own grave."

"Thanks, Jeff. This clarity is really helpful."

"So, you would like to do a marker for your father?"

"Yes. One matching the rest. How ought I proceed? I am suspecting that E. Wunderlich Granite did the work when Dad had the stone done for his parents."

"Yes, Father. I checked into that. Call them and they will work with you."

"Is there anything else, Jeff?

"Yes, Father. You probably should talk with Rick Cabay at St. Joe's cemetery about the stone replacement and what to do with the marker your stepmother had placed. You don't have to do it right away, but it would be a good idea to do it before the new stone is ready to be set. I am sure Rick will work with you."

The process of ordering the gravestone took some months. E. Wunderlich Granite had to go out to the graves to see what was there regarding granite type and stone design. They needed to assess as well what resetting Grandma and Grandpa Papesh's stone required, since I decided to do that at the same time. I ultimately ordered a flush-to-the-ground St. Cloud grey granite stone with an IHS upper left. The stone was to have on it Dad's name and his birth and death years. Under his name, in quotes, would be his nickname "Mickey." In the upper margin, center, would be the word *Father*. In the lower margin, center, would be the words *Funeral Director*. I also asked that the stone be set in a concrete bed and frame so that it matched Grandma and Grandpa's reset stone in appearance and would not sink as the years passed.

When Wunderlich informed me it was ready, I contacted Rick Cabay at St. Joe's. "It's nice to talk to you, Father," Rick told me. "I knew your dad. We worked together on many funerals. He was a nice man and a good funeral director. Tops in my book."

"Thanks, Rick. I appreciate hearing that. Thank you very much. I am calling about replacing the stone on Dad's grave from the military one that's there to one that matches the family stone."

"You want to replace the stone Lillian had set there?" Taken off-guard by the immediacy and exactness of Rick's memory, I instantly remembered that news traveled fast throughout the Slovenian community and I needed to remain sensitive to that.

"Yes, Rick. Frankly, there has been family stress around the marker because Lil went ahead with the military one without checking things out with my brother and me. So, we want to right a mistake here."

"Oh, okay, Father. I see." I thought I sensed some reserve. Might his family be intermarried with Lil's? Not sure. Quite possibly.

"So, I understand, Rick, that the new stone is ready and coming from E. Wunderlich Granite," I plowed on. "And I just wanted to alert you that I would like the stone they are installing to replace what's there."

"What do you want done with the military marker, Father?"

I was thrown. I had failed to think that through. "I would simply like to have it removed, Rick, and disposed of. Can you destroy it?"

"Not really, Father. The government paid for it. How about putting it at the foot of the grave?"

"Gee, Rick. I would prefer not. Can you dispose of it?" I had not expected difficulty. I had assumed his work maintaining the cemetery was simply and only that, neglecting to think through the relationships side of his managing a parish cemetery.

"Father, does Lillian know you are doing this?" That brought me up short and opened wide a door that I preferred to leave mostly closed. I instantly saw how very narrow-minded my suppositions had been.

"No, Rick," I replied, feeling compelled to be honest. "But I talked this out with Jeff Dames and understand that legally I am within my rights as eldest son to have the marker replaced." I wanted to be clear and firm without being defensive.

"That's true, Father, but I really don't want to have trouble here at the cemetery when she sees the change-out." The Slovenian community was not only small and tight-knit, but more-than-a-little forthright. He knew his folks. "So, why don't I put the military marker at the foot of the grave."

Rick desired peace. I wanted to be kind and respectful while remaining within my rights. "Rick, I prefer that you somehow dispose of the military marker, but I will leave what you do to your best judgment. You have larger considerations, I see." That felt honest to me, and generously respectful under the circumstances. Rick didn't deserve to be in anyone's crosshairs.

"Thank you, Father. I will take care of it." I admired his discretion. In-between the lines, I felt certain the military marker would be set at the foot of the grave. "We work with Wunderlich's all the time, Father. No problem."

Wunderlich's set Dad's stone marker and reset Grandma and Grandpa's sinking marker in December 2003. Gloria sent pictures. She approved.

Rick indeed set the military marker at the foot of Dad's grave. I decided to let that go for now. I also decided to no longer take initiative in relationship with Lil.

Through the time of the grave marker preparation and setting, two realities emerged that affirmed the process.

Lil, I learned through Gloria, had a boyfriend. Lil met Ed, who was from New York and three years older than she, while Dad was in the nursing home. Ed's wife had been in the nursing home during a time overlapping with Dad, and she had died. Ed and Lil marked 2002 as the beginning of their relationship. Ed and Lil ate and traveled together, and Ed eventually moved into Lil and Dad's Venice home. Excited by the new relationship, and presuming friendship with Gloria, Lil shared with Gloria freely about the good times they were enjoying together, their travels, and Ed's family. Lil told Gloria she had no desire to marry again, mostly to protect her pension. Like Dad, Lil evidently needed "a squeeze" for her to feel life was complete. Our family, Gloria especially, felt none-too-happy about what Lil so cheerily reported.

The family's relationship with Lil also hit a snag over our feelings about the family burial plot. Gloria wrote in April 2003, the lava of her anger oozing off the paper, "I still can't figure out why Tina's ashes are on my mom and dad's lots. Unless I have it wrong, I don't remember Tina in my family." She wrote the following September, the lava becoming a decided flow, "I know your dad never wanted what Lil did… I really had a fit. My mom and dad were very special people and they don't deserve what happened. Even my family doesn't think it's right."

Roger and I agreed with Gloria and knew that by trespassing on Gloria's sensibilities, Lil flirted with blunt confrontation. The only question was when it would occur.

In early August 2004, on my way back to Minnesota from an extended visit in Colorado, I decided to swing through Illinois to check the gravestone work and have a Merichka's poorboy. I arranged an early breakfast with Gloria on Joliet's west side.

"Well," Gloria said when we got comfortable in the booth. "I have a story for you."

Gloria reported that Lil had come up to Illinois a month earlier to visit her mother. She and Lynn, who lived in Illinois, met with Gloria and her daughter Jackie for lunch. Conversation passed pleasantly until dessert time.

"Well," Lil began. "I suppose you have heard about our trouble with Fr. Mike." She evidently had only just seen the new marker on the grave during this visit.

"What trouble with Fr. Mike, Lil?" Gloria asked. "He's in Minnesota and you're in Florida! What trouble could you have with him?" Characteristically playing it coy, Gloria left the direction of the conversation up to Lil. Used to being in trouble, as she put it, Gloria at least made the effort to avoid it.

"I mean about the graves," Lil said. She then went on to explain that she feared that I would exhume Tina's ashes and move her and so had engaged a lawyer to check out her legal rights. She also complained about the new marker.

When Lil finished, silence thundered. She had just given Gloria the opening for which she had longed. Gloria took it.

"Lil, after my dad died in 1971, I gave the rights to the family graves to Mike. They had been in my name, but I gave them to Mike. He got two graves. I didn't ask anything for them. I was happy to do it. I did that, Lil, because he was a Papesh and I am a Farkas. I am going to be buried with the Farkases. The way I see it, Lil, Tina is a Bozich. She is not a Papesh. Tina should be buried with the Bozich's, not the Papeshes."

Wide-eyed, Lil squirmed, then immediately turned to her daughter. "Well, Lynn, I guess it's time to go."

They got up, grabbed their purses, and headed to the cash register. Lil and Lynn exchanged cool pleasantries with Gloria and Jackie on the way out. Gloria's plain opinion, however, likely struck Lil as a little too clear.

When I heard the punch line of the story, I felt gleeful. "Boy, Gloria, do I thank you for that!" I told her. "You saved me a lot of trouble by being so straightforward and sticking up for the family like that. Thank you, thank you, thank you. I am so glad you did that!"

"Mike, Tina just shouldn't be there," Gloria rejoined. "I just wanted Lil to know it's not right. And you're welcome."

"I don't think it's reasonable to do anything more about it, Gloria. I don't think it's right to disturb the dead. We just have to live with what is. But I am so glad she knows how we feel."

"I agree with that. I'm not sure my telling her makes any difference anyway, Mike," Gloria said, "but I thought she needed to know."

Lil continued her relationship with Gloria intermittently. She had the block-headed insensitivity, however, or perhaps thoughtless superficiality, to continue to write and gush with Gloria about her relationship with Ed, their cruises, Ed's family, and how happy she was. Lil clearly failed to understand Gloria.

Gloria shared with me her response to Lil's chatter in a letter in February 2005. "All I have to say about that whole things is – AMEN –."

Gloria and I never wrote or spoke about Lillian again.

Eleven years later, in June 2014, Mom and I traveled together from Colorado to Joliet to meet with her sister, Joanie, who had flown up from Florida. We gathered to enjoy one another's company, tour old family haunts, and celebrate Mom and Joanie's mid-June birthdays. Before leaving for the trip, I called Rick Cabay at St. Joe's cemetery and asked him to remove the military marker from the bottom of Dad's grave. I told him I would come in a few days to pick it up. We set a date and time. Rick asked no questions.

On a lovely June evening, I stopped by the cemetery, with Mom and Joanie in the car, to say a prayer at Dad's grave and trim around his and Grandma and Grandpa Papesh's headstones. I noted gratefully the earthen square in the grass at the foot of Dad's grave where the military marker had been. I also noticed two military markers on the adjacent grave, one for Tina, one for Lil.

After finishing the trimming, I drove over to the cemetery maintenance shed to meet Rick and pick up Dad's bronze marker. I told him I was happy to finally meet him and extended him my thanks for all he had done. He said he was happy to meet me and once again made kind remarks about his work with Dad. He asked no questions. I offered no reflections.

With Mom and Joanie still in the car, I drove out of St. Joe's cemetery and two miles through the Slovenian neighborhood to the Des Plaines River, what Grandma Papesh always referred to as "the canal." Making a right on Bluff Street at the foot of the Ruby Street bridge on the west side of the river, I turned left off the blacktop onto gravel and scrub grass. I swung the car in a circle and backed-up toward the river wall.

I excused myself from Mom and Joanie, opened the car trunk and took up the heavy bronze marker. I walked with it twenty feet to the river and stood up on the concrete wall. The house my great-grandfather Papesh built, the house where my grandfather and father had been raised, sat a half-block west below the setting sun. Across the river, just a half-block east, stood the remains of the steel mill where Great-Grandpa Papesh, Great-Grandpa Vesel and Grandpa Papesh had all worked to support the family. The twin towers of the Slovenian parish church, three blocks farther southeast, gleamed rose-silver in the dusk.

I soaked in the view, realizing that Dad saw it very often, daily for most of his life. From here he walked to church and school, here sat his neighborhood, here he played as a boy, by here he drove to his funeral home and to Mass and parish meetings, and by here he passed for the last time on his way to the cemetery thirteen years before.

As I beheld the church towers, I prayed, "Eternal rest grant unto him, O Lord, and let perpetual light shine upon him. May he rest in peace." I let the bronze marker slide through my hands to plunge into the river. "May his soul, and the souls of all the faithful departed, through the mercy of God, rest in peace. Amen."